JUST HOW MUCH SCRAP LUMBER DOES A MAN NEED TO SAVE?

Janet Letnes Martin

and

Suzann (Johnson) Nelson

CARAGANA PRESS

CARAGANA PRESS
BOX 396
HASTINGS, MN 55033

Printed in the United States of America

Published by Caragana Press
Box 396, Hastings, Minnesota 55033

ISBN 1-886627-08-8

FIRST EDITION

Cover Design: Joe Gillaspie
              Hastings, MN

Runestone and Scrap Lumber Drawings:
                Art Nordstrom
                Hastings, MN

Cave Man Cartoon: Scott Calton
                  Prescott, WI

Printer: Sentinel Printing
          St. Cloud, MN

Photographs: Friends, families and foes

DEDICATION

This book is dedicated
to the men in our families
who, by saving Scrap Lumber,
gave us good material
for writing this MANual.

TO OUR READERS:

This MANual is the result of an informal survey conducted among our female friends in the summer of 1999. The survey question was: "Just how much Scrap Lumber does a man need to save?" Ninety-nine percent of the females responded, "None of it!"

We thought it only fair to ask the men the same question: "Just how much Scrap Lumber does a man need to save?" So we did. Ninety-nine percent of the males responded, "All of it!"

We weren't trying to start the battle of the sexes, but after the responses we received, we knew we were onto something big. Using our usual research methods of coffee, computers, coffee and more coffee, we dug and explored in depth the complex issue of "Why do men save Scrap Lumber?" We're happy to report that this MANual sheds some light on this age-old problem which was never discussed at Augsburg College in our history, economics, psychology or religion classes.

By reading this MANual you will realize that as long as there are men, trees and lumber yards on this earth, there will be Scrap Lumber heaps. No, they will not become nostalgic things like cream separators or threshing machines that are oddly, but neatly, parked in yards and fields as endearing monuments to times past. Scrap Lumber piles are a species onto their own. Scrap Lumber heaps are like dandelions that sprout up all over, and no matter how hard you try to get rid of them, they grow, flourish, spread and take over everything. Nothing kills them. They are like wisdom teeth or an appendix, i.e., things that aren't particularly useful and generally cause trouble.

The truth is this: Men will continue to go to the lumber yard to buy new stuff and, by buying new stuff, they will create even more Scrap Lumber piles.

However, all is not lost for us women. By creating more Scrap Lumber piles, men have given us the opportunity to gather enough material to write this book. (When we say "gather enough material," we're not talking about buying more fabric to sew a gathered skirt. That's a different book that a brave man should write.)

We have some good news for the men, too! We need lots of paper produced so we can continue to publish books about your quirks. So go ahead and keep your chainsaws buzzing so we can be assured that enough paper will be produced to print the next two books in our MANual trilogy, "Just How Much Scrap Iron Does a Man Need to Collect," and "Just How Many Tires Does a Man Need to Kick?"

Enjoy this!

Those Lutheran Ladies,
Janet Letnes Martin & Suzann Nelson

P.S. We know that after reading this MANual, you'll want to order our coordinating Scrap Lumber teeshirts and hats. The order blank is in back of this book.

TABLE of CONTENTS

THE PAST:

THE PRESENT:

THE FUTURE:

CHAPTER ONE

WE CAN BLAME NOAH

Mt. Ararat Lutheran Church

WE CAN BLAME NOAH

Saving Scrap Lumber can be traced all the way back to Noah. The story goes something like this.

Once upon a time God told Noah to build an ark because He was going to flood the earth and destroy everyone and everything, including the Lutheran Church but he would spare Noah, his family, and two of every species of animal including mosquitoes, skunks and aardvarks. He said to Noah, "Hurry up and build the ark or you'll be in hot water, too." So Noah obeyed. He said to his boys, Ham, Shem and Japheth, "Ham, you take the pickup over to the lumber yard and get some Gopher wood. Make sure you get enough cubits so we don't have to waste time and gas making another trip to town. Shem, you can start sawing it up as soon as your brother is back with it, and Japheth, you nail 'er up when Shem's done sawing it."

So Noah and the boys worked around the clock like they did in threshing season. The women worked even harder making all the food for the trip. They canned sauce, beet pickles, rutabagas, herring and all sorts of other things. They rolled out flat bread until their arms ached. They made dozens of rock cookies and packed them in Nash Finch coffee jars. When they had finished making the food, they carefully packed it all in cardboard boxes and peach crates, and sealed the boxes and crates with adhesive tape and string. They used one of Noah's carpenter's pencils and wrote on each box what was in it. The women finished their work before the men were done with their work because they didn't stop for lunch or snoozing. They just kept going.

The men finally finished the Ark and got the animals herded in just in time. When everybody and everything that was supposed to be in the Ark was in the Ark, they had time to sit and think, eat and sleep, play Rook and Chinese checkers, and listen to the rain pelt the Ark. After a few days Noah was getting a little bored and restless. He said to his sons, "Hey, where did you boys put the Scrap Lumber that was left over? I got time to stack and sort it." The boys fought and argued and blamed each other for forgetting it. Finally Noah said, "Looks like none of you are going to be above board about it. I'm sure it's floating all the way to China by now." Noah was right. When the Ark landed and they got out to look around, the Scrap Lumber was no where in sight. They dismantled the Ark and built a Lutheran Church with the lumber. There was some Scrap Lumber left over, and Noah kept it in a safe dry place with his Lutheran Brotherhood Insurance Policy until he died. His funeral was at the Mount Ararat Lutheran Church, the edifice he had built with the lumber from the old Ark.

Ham, Shem and Japheth sold Noah's Scrap Lumber at an auction, cashed in his Lutheran Brotherhood life insurance policy, bought themselves new cabin cruisers, and took off for greener pastures. Ham went to Yugoslavia and died of e-coli from some undercooked ham hocks. Japheth ended up in Japan and died from some kind of overdose. Shem went to live in a cave near the *Hardanger Fjord* in Norway. He lived to a ripe old age.

This is most certainly true.

CHAPTER TWO

SLIVER,
THE PATHETIC CAVEMAN
AND HIS SCRAP LUMBER

Opening to Sliver's Cave
Note: After his wives left he
never bothered to clean up
his junk. He lived like a pig.

SLIVER, THE PATHETIC CAVEMAN, AND HIS SCRAP LUMBER

Once upon a time Shem took up shipbuilding around the *Hardanger Fjord* because it was in his blood. He died of hard work and old age when he was way up in his nineties. After he died his son, Shim, took over the business. Shim was a hard worker, but died when the side of his boat collapsed on him while he was trying to shim it up.

Shim's son, Sliver, who had never learned how to work hard because his father and grandfather had paved the way to fame and fortune for him in the family shipbuilding business, rejected the Lutheran faith and spent his days collecting and sorting Scrap Lumber and writing poetry on cave walls. When the spirit moved him he hunted big game, fished for walleyes, smoked weeds and beat on drums. When Sliver got bored, he roamed around and kicked women and stray dogs who got in his way.

His Mrs., on the other hand, kept busy from sunup to sundown rubbing sticks together to start fires, skinning animals, drying fish, making pelts, rendering lard, picking chokecherries, shelling nuts, taking slivers out of kids and cleaning her cave.

When the kids were old enough to be out of the cave and on their own, Sliver's Mrs. came out of the darkness. She saw the light, said "enough's enough," grabbed the pelts and the Scrap Lumber and the canning jars, and left the cave for good. She, with the help of Habitat for Humanity, built herself a nice little rambler and used the pelts for wall-to-wall carpeting in her living room. She gathered berries and nuts and became a vegetarian. She survived nicely into old age, even though she became hard of hearing and had a little lumbago.

After his Mrs. was gone, Sliver went hunting and found himself a young woman and married her. It didn't take her more than a week of living with him before she saw the light in the woods and took off.

He tried to chase her down but she was younger, faster and brighter than Sliver. She left him choking in her dust. Now he was all alone. Because he had never learned how to cook or fend for himself, he ended up eating raw meat and rotten fish that had washed up on shore. He died from either trichinosis or from choking on a fish bone. We're just not quite sure how he died, nor do we care.

We know this is most certainly true because archeologists and college kids from St. Olaf College who were digging in the *Hardanger Fjord* caves found Scrap Lumber heaps on his cave floor and detailed drawings and writings on his cave walls.

Historians who received grant money when the Democrats were in control translated the following writings and drawings from his cave walls.

This is most certainly true.

Sliver's Scrap Lumber pile before
his Trophy wife took off with it.

SLIVER'S CAVE DRAWINGS

TRANSLATION OF SLIVER'S CAVE DRAWING

Me woman took scrap piece of me good oak and hid it in wall crevice. Me found it. Her admit her was going to decoupage it. Me got angry and hit her over head with it, but her didn't bleed much. Her left cave and never came back. Then Me bagged me a trophy wife, but her couldn't cook so me hit her. Her didn't bleed nothing, just bump on head. Her left and took all me Scrap Lumber, even me good oak piece me hit me first wife with. Now me had no thing to remember me first wife by. Me tried to hunt her down, but her run faster than deer. Me now alone and me don't have no Scrap Lumber to look at or sort. Women took everything from me that matters in life, and now Sheriff even questioned me. Now me, Sliver, left alone to write on wall and tell me story about me evil women.

CHAPTER THREE

THE VIKINGS AND THEIR SCRAP LUMBER: THE TALE OF ERIK THE RED OAK AND LEIF THE LUCKY

(Left to Right)

Sigrid Nilsdatter, Leif's Mrs.;

Ingrid Larsdatter, Sigrid's friend;

Eric the Red Oak;

Ruby the Wild Rose;

Leif the Lucky.

(This picture was taken before Lucy the Lucky was in the picture.)

THE VIKINGS AND THEIR SCRAP LUMBER: THE TALE OF ERIC THE RED OAK AND LEIF THE LUCKY

Once upon a time after Sliver died, his red-headed hot-tempered grandson, Eric the Red Oak, stole a boat, got the heck out of *Hardanger* and took off for Iceland.

He hung around Iceland until he was snagged by Ruby the Wild Rose, a good-looking, blonde, seemingly obedient, woman who knew how to cook. She promised the minister she'd take care of her man. After they had been married about a week, she turned on him and refused to clean, cook or take care of him. All she did was nag, nag, nag — day in and day out — until one day he couldn't take it anymore. He went out and got drunk, staggered home, and grabbed the bottle of Avon's "To a Wild Rose" perfume that he had bought her when he was wooing her. He poured the whole thing down the hole in the outhouse which wasn't really outside, but a little room off the kitchen. He glared at her and said, "There goes my Wild Rose."

Then, Ruby the Wild Rose, calmly picked up Eric the Red Oak's biggest and most prized piece of red oak Scrap Lumber and with her bare hands split it in two right in front of his eyes and said, "Eric, there goes the red oak." She continued to split his prized red oak Scrap Lumber piece until all that was left was a pile of splinters. In a calm, firm voice she said, "Now take your red oak splinters and get out of here or I'm calling the cops." Eric, knowing full well he couldn't win for losing, picked up his splinters of red oak, jumped in his boat, and went to Greenland.

By the time he reached Greenland he was tired and hungry, but he also got lucky. A woman named Lucy the Lucky took him in, bedded him down, fed him up and nursed his ego. She could cook and she didn't nag so he married her.

They had a son named Leif, and more children but they were nothing to speak of or write home about. When Leif was about Confirmation Age, his dad, Eric the Red, died in bed of rotten *rømmegrøt*. Lucy and Leif dumped his body in the ocean because there were no trees in Greenland to build a casket, and it was cheaper than a full-blown funeral.

Leif the Lucky Ericsson married Sigrid Nilsdatter and she put up with more than most woman would. He was born with ants in his pants and one day, out of the blue, he decided to take off with his other married buddies in his dad's old boat for a little adventure and greener pastures. Truthfully speaking, Greenland was as green of a pasture as you could find any place on the earth, but didn't have trees. It didn't have forests, and it didn't have Scrap Lumber piles. So Leif and his buddies loaded up the old boat with Dainty Moore Stew, Spam and beer and off they went into the wild blue yonder.

After a few days they landed off the coast of Maine. The land was so full of trees and forests they couldn't see either the forest for the trees or the trees for the forest. They set up camp, filled their bellies with food, drank some beer, belched a bunch, fished a little, felled some trees, and fought with each other over Scrap Lumber piles. Some of them even died by the ax.

In no time at all they ran out of food. None of them knew how to cook and many of them starved to death. The remaining survivors decided they better beat it back home or they'd be history too. When these prodigal sons returned to Greenland they sure didn't get much sympathy from their women. "Serves them right," said Sigrid Nilsdatter, (Leif Ericsson's Mrs.) to Ingrid Larsdatter when they were both hanging up their men's wet underwear on the community clothesline.

After they'd been fed well, fattened up and felt back to health, Leif the Lucky and the lucky survivors who made it back in one piece bragged about their exploits and told fish stories about Scrap Lumber that were passed down, sometimes to the children of the third and fourth generations.

Eventually these tales, or sagas as they were later called, were written down on lava rocks by their great-great- great-great-grandchildren who had learned Runic writing while they were Reading for the Minister. Some of these lava stones, which were latter called Runestones, eventually showed up partially buried under trees near Alexandria, MN, and one of these Runestones was found 950 years later by a couple of Concordia College choir students who needed to earn some money so they could go to Oslo with the choir to sing for King Olav.

The Concordia College students, Ronald Peterson and Ingrid Iverson, were both farm kids who were used to working hard so in the summer they agreed to pick rocks and haul them on

stoneboats for Sverre Olson whose farm was near
Kensington, MN. (Kensington is just down the road
apiece from Alexandria, MN.)

One day when they were busy working it was
getting about time for noon dinner so the two sat
down in unison (like they did in the choir) on some
rocks under a grove of trees with their "termoses,"
lunch buckets and water jugs. Just as Ronald was
opening the wax paper which was folded around
his dried beef sandwich, he looked down and no-
ticed some writing on the big stone he was sitting
on. "*Neiman, du da*," he said, "What in the world
does this say, then?"

Ingrid Iverson, who was majoring in Norwegian
and got in the choir because her grandfather was
one of the founding fathers of the C-400 Club, put
down her Watkins Nectar jug, looked at the stone
and said, "Ya, this is *Norsk* all right. I think we
might have something here, then. We better put it
on the stoneboat and haul it to the Runestone
Museum in Alexandria. They could use a new
stone." So they did just that. Then Ingrid translated the writings on the stone for the museum.
People came from miles around and from bigwig
places like Harvard to sit and think, wonder and
marvel, and argue and pontificate about the stone.

When Ingrid and Ronald went to Norway with
the choir to sing for King Olav, he had already
heard about their discovery of the Runestone so he
met with them, gave them each a medal, and said,
"Ya, *tusen takk for alt*." (A thousand thanks for
everything.)

This is most certainly true.

RUNIC WRITING ON STONE

Now this is what was written on the stone:

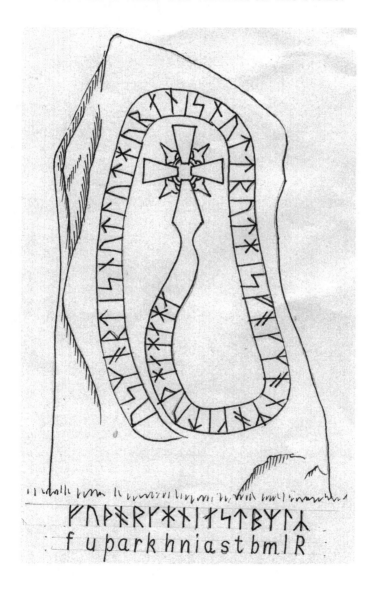

f u þ a r k h n i a s t b m l R

SINGLE SWINGER THE RED
BEFORE HE MARRIED
AGNES THE LONELY

THE SAGA OF SINGLE SWINGER THE RED AND HIS SCRAP LUMBER

Once upon a time far up north there lived a man called Single Swinger the Red who was a distant relative of Leif the Lucky, and nine begats down from Oldefar the Bushy who was a carpenter by trade and liked to do other things with his hands.

Because Oldefar the Bushy's mother had grown up in the Great Depression of 1540, Oldefar learned the wisdom of being frugal and passed the trait down from one begat to another. Well, when Single Swinger the Red was banished from Grant County, MN for slaying He-Man the Horrible with nothing but a secondhand *Huskvarna* chainsaw, Single knew that to survive the bad winters, the telemarketers and the Mormon Door-knockers, he would have to venture over the border where one could see farther. Thus it was that in 1954 Single Swinger the Red found himself bagging groceries at the Piggly-Wiggly checkout in Wahpeton, ND.

It was here that he had time to rest up, shave and plot strategy. Because so many Norwegian immigrant clans had summer *"stevner"* or reunions at the Wahpeton School of Science, Single thought to himself, "Oh ya, then. This would be a good place to reconnect with my roots and get on with life." Thus it was that he went to the *Hallinglag* Reunion in 1955 and met Agnes the

Lonely from near Canton, SD.

Agnes the Lonely had learned a thing or two from her mother, Florence the Frugal, who — like Oldefar the Bushy's mother — had also survived a Great Depression, albeit 390 years and many begats, kings, railroads, *lutefisk* suppers, church cookbooks and U.S. Presidents later. With this union of Agnes and Single there began the Great Collect and Salvage Union, the likes of which this world has not seen since.

Drawing upon his family's history of pilfering, plundering, protecting, persevering and preserving, Single Swinger the Red began to store up things of value to trade with the Swedes, Irish and Republicans once he reached his eventual destination of Canton-to-be-with-Agnes, SD. With his used *Huskvarna* he chopped down anything that smacked of wood and brandished his used *Huskvarna* as a weapon to get the less-than-vocal North Dakotans to haul his Scrap Lumber to the nearest train depot.

In the days of the "Winnipeg Flyer of the Great Northern," the North Dakotans hauled load upon load of fresh Scrap Lumber to Canton: embarking in Fargo, transferring it to stockcars and hotrods, and debarking it along the way. They also added whatever Scrap Lumber they could pilfer from farmers who wanted to clean up their farmyards now that all the Scrap Iron had been sent off a decade earlier for the War Effort.

Thus it was that Single Swinger changed his name to Mr. Clean of Canton, SD and was given the St. Olaf Medal by the King of Norway for ridding immigrant descendants' homesteads of blight.

Agnes and her man lived many happy years upon the prairie where he collected and stacked Scrap Lumber and where she dusted both the Scrap Lumber and the church parlors twice a year. They were as clean, happy and wholesome as any scavengers could be until 1958 when wanderlust again attacked and plagued them and they ventured back to Wahpeton for yet another *stevne* and to have a Fudgesickle at the Piggly-Wiggly. (He saved both wooden sticks from the Fudgesickles to add to his Scrap Lumber pile).

With that adventure back to Wahpeton — combined with Mr. Clean's carving of limbless dolls from Scrap Lumber and Agnes's *Hardangersøm* using string too short to save of-which-they-had-a-plenty — they were content and lived out the duration of their lives near Canton Township 54-26, Section 3, SD, until Thor and bloodclots called them home.

Thus, the Scrap Lumber was given to St. Sonja's Lutheran on the Prairie for new, great big, many-holed, fits-your-Scandinavian-modesty outhouses at the back of the cemetery behind the lilac bushes, and the Great Collect and Salvage Union was abolished.

This is most certainly true.

(Written down by an unknown Lutheran author in the 21st Century and translated by Egil Eagle the Equestrian and Egg-Gatherer from Evansville, also just down the road apiece from Alexandria, MN.)

CHAPTER FOUR

COLUMBUS SAILED THE OCEAN BLUE AND CAME BACK WITH NARY A PIECE OF SCRAP LUMBER

Columbus showing off his new
clothes before he set sail.

COLUMBUS SAILED THE OCEAN BLUE AND CAME BACK WITH NARY A PIECE OF SCRAP LUMBER

Once upon a time King Ferdinand and Queen Isabella of Spain called a young sailor named Columbus into their court.

"Hey," King Ferdinand said. "We just got a call from the Pope in Rome. He said there was a rumor going through the grapevine that some of his renegade distant Lutheran cousins from Greenland had discovered a new land and it was loaded with lumber. He ordered us to command you to build some ships, get a crew of Catholics together, get over there and get some of that lumber before the Lutherans take it all."

Queen Isabella, who never took a back seat to her man, continued, "He wants you to convert the natives to Catholicism and build some churches while you're there. Here's some money to get the ships built. But, before you go, write up a mission or a vision statement so we have something in on paper to show the Pope in exchange for the purgatory money he gave us." She thought for a minute and whispered into Columbus's ear, "If there are any good deals on gold chains, pick up a few. I'll pay you back later."

So Columbus obeyed even though his Ma wrote the mission and vision stuff for him. He and a bunch of Spanish sailors built *The Nina, The Pinta* and *The Santa Maria* and set sail. Right away they ran into trouble. The winds came up, the sea got rough, and they washed up on the shores of San Salvador. The natives there treated Columbus and gang like royalty as soon as they staggered down the gangplank on their sea legs. It was party-hearty with rum and cokes until the wee hours of the morning.

After they had been there a couple weeks, Columbus said to Rumhead, the Chief Chieftain, "I don't know if any one told you, but we came here looking for some lumber to bring back to Spain. I don't see many trees here. Can you give us directions to a place up North where some Lutheran Viking Greenlanders supposedly settled?" Rumhead, the Chief Chieftain, said, "Sure as shootin' can. Just go North for a couple days, then go due West, turn left about a mile past Skogen's skerry, and you'll run right into it. Believe me, you can't miss it. It's just up the shore and down the road apiece."

So Columbus and his men loaded up their ship with cases of rum and 24-packs of Coca-Cola that Rumhead and his people had given them as a parting gifts and they took off. After a couple days the winds came up, the seas got rough and they washed up on the shores of Jamaica.

The natives of Jamaica, were just as nice and friendly as the natives of San Salvador had been. They fed Columbus's folks food smothered in Jamaica Jerky and filled their Tupperware glasses with Bahama Mama's. They stayed a couple more weeks and then Columbus said to the natives, "No, we best get going." The natives gave them cases of Jamaica Jerky as a parting gift. They loaded it up on their ships, traded e-mail addresses and set sail. This time they weren't so lucky.

After three days of rough water, they sailed right into the Bermuda Triangle and lost *The Nina* to the deep blue seas. They all jumped on *The Pinta* and *The Santa Maria,* but *The Pinta* took on water from all the weight and she went down. Then they loaded everything and everybody and the jerky on *The Santa Maria.* It was about to sink but, lo and behold, it floated until it came ashore on a sparsely inhabited island called Cuba. They knew the Good Lord and Christopher's navigating abilities had saved them so the first thing they did was craft St. Christopher Medals out of Scrap Iron and hung them around their necks as a reminder of their good fortune.

Their luck continued with more good fortune. This island had some good stogies and a few trees. They chopped the trees down and built replicas of the *Nina* and *Pinta.* They loaded *The Santa Maria* and the new boats *The Nina II* and *The Pinta II* with the rum and coke, Jamaica Jerky and Bahama Mama mix. They each lit up a big stogie and they headed back to Spain.

When they got back to Spain, Columbus told Ferdie and Bella the good news. Not only had they and all their ships made it back safely, but they had also found the forest the Viking Lutherans had raided.

The bad news was that there was no Scrap Lumber to bring back because they used it all up building Catholic Churches.

Columbus gave the King and Queen the gifts from the natives and mixed King Ferdinand a rum and coke. Ferdinand mellowed out fast. Columbus fixed a Bahama Mama for Queen Isabella and gave her a St. Christopher Medal that he had forged out of Scrap Iron. He had spray painted it gold so she would think it was the real thing. She fell for it hook, line, and sinker and believed, until her dying day, it was 18-karat gold.

Ferdinand and Isabella called the Pope collect in the middle of the day and told him the good news. The Pope made Christopher the Patron Saint of Travelers, ordered his craftsmen to make St. Christopher statues, and had his papal scribes write books detailing Christopher's discovery of America and about his success at converting the natives to Catholicism.

This is most certainly true.

CHAPTER FIVE

THE IMMIGRANTS AND THEIR SCRAP LUMBER: WHAT GOES AROUND, COMES AROUND

Immigrant Ole Olson in front of one of his
"lean-tos" he built from Scrap Lumber.

The Scrap Lumber pile in front of Ole's
"lean-tos" that set Lena off on her rampage.

THE IMMIGRANTS AND THEIR SCRAP LUMBER: WHAT GOES AROUND COMES AROUND

Once upon a time, about 350 years after Columbus had told the biggest fib in all of history, the countries of Norway, Sweden, Denmark, Finland, and Germany were running out of land and trees for their people.

Through the grapevine the people of these countries heard that one could find all the land, lakes and Lutherans, they could ever dream of seeing in the State of Minnesota.

The United States government had enacted the Homestead Act which entitled an immigrant to 160 acres of free land if he cleaned it up and made it tillable in five years. Upon hearing this news Ole Olson said to his wife, Lena, "Let's go. It sounds like the Holy Land to me. Why *yust tink* of all the Scrap Lumber piles I could have." So Ole used the last of his Scrap Lumber pile and made a trunk for the trip. Lena really didn't want to go but she was Ole's wife and she had promised "whether thou go'est, I will go" so she was between a rock and a hard place and really had no choice. So she helped Ole fill the trunk with a few tools, a spinning wheel, a little bit of cotton material, some flat bread, a little coffee, two scatter rugs, hollyhock seeds and a Bible. They shook hands with their parents and off they went to Northern Minnesota.

However, as they say, the grass isn't always greener on the other side. It was true that Minnesota had lots of land and lakes and was overrun with Lutherans as they had been told, but Minnesota also had other things that weren't so good— things like isolation, mosquitoes, humid summers, dust bowls, grasshopper infestations and peddlers coming down the driveway.

But Ole and Lena were tough and they were strong and they survived. They toiled and they sweat while raising cows, kids, corn and barns. Ole cleared the trees and in no time at all he built himself a regular red barn, loafing barn, farrowing barn, turkey barn and a pole barn. He built a grease shed, tool shed, wood shed, shearing shed and a machine shed. Then he built a pump house, milk house, well house, engine house, brooder house, bunk house and a three-holer outhouse. For Lena he built a little house and a summer kitchen, and a playhouse for the kids. That's not all! He built a root cellar, storm cellar and a fruit cellar. In addition he put up a potato warehouse, blacksmith shop, feedlot, corncrib, granary, chicken coop, sheep pen, milking parlor, trench silo and a whole bunch of "lean-tos".

With each new building, Ole's Scrap Lumber piles grew and spread and took over every spare inch in and around all his buildings and on the grounds. When Ole was done clearing his land and building his farm he was as content as a cud-chewing cow grazing on clover to spend his time drinking coffee and sorting and resorting his Scrap Lumber piles. Life was good for him, but not for his kids or his dear wife, Lena.

When Ole and Lena's kids had graduated from 8th grade they all left the folks, the farm and the Scrap Lumber piles for the bright lights and action of the Twin Cities. Meanwhile, Lena — who was going through the change but certainly wasn't as stiff in mind, soul or body as Ole — secretly envied her kids and began to brood. Why, Ole wouldn't even take her to town Saturday night for the drawing. So Lena sulked and became withdrawn. Ole knew something was up, but it wasn't something he would talk to her about, so he didn't. Lena didn't talk to Ole about it either because she knew after all these years there was no way he could or would follow her train of thought. So Lena had no way out but to let her feelings go deep inside and fester like the pointer finger does when a nasty sliver is lodged under the skin. Eventually the infection (or pus, as it was called in those days) on a pointer finger breaks open, and there's no way of stopping it and that's precisely what happened to Lena.

Whether it was a hormone imbalance, wanderlust, something in her blood or something in the air or water no one will ever know. But early one summer morning when Ole was drinking coffee and reading a farm magazine on the front porch, Lena walked by him and down the steps with a full garbage can in hand. He thought she was taking it to the burning barrel, but a few seconds later when he happened to look up he saw that she had stopped dead in her tracks, dropped the garbage can, run over to the grease shed and got the kerosene can. Then she went over to Ole's biggest Scrap Lumber pile, poured the kerosene on it, pulled a farmer's match out of her apron pocket and lit it. Then she went to the next pile and did the same thing.

After watching four of his prized Scrap Lumber piles go up in flames Ole became so distraught he couldn't get a word out edgewise. So he did the next best thing. He got up off his chair to run after her and shake some sense into her, but he fell over and he died before he could make it down the porch steps. Lena mourned a little bit but not too much. He wasn't even cold before she had an auction and sold everything that Ole had worked so hard to accumulate.

Lena moved to town and took up card-playing and square dancing with Hank, the furniture store owner from town. They got married and kept her house in town. She had quite a bit of money left over from the auction so she bought a little cabin up North where they could socialize and fish in the summer. The following winter she thought, what the heck, a gal only lives once, so she bought a trailer house in Arizona where they could drink peach daiquiris and play shuffleboard in the winter.

Everything was peachy keen for a couple years, but then Lena's Lutheran Confirmation Guilt came home to roost. She developed acid reflux, an ulcer, and died in the desert. Hank didn't bother to bring her home to Minnesota. He buried her on the spot and within a few weeks he took up with a much younger woman named Bunny.

Shortly thereafter Hank, the furniture store owner, died and Bunny hit the jackpot and got everything but the kitchen sink which she didn't want anyway. Bunny sold the house and cottage up North which she had inherited, but had never seen. She sold the trailer house in Arizona, and she took the money and moved to California where she found a man much younger than Hank. His name was Lyle and his hobby was collecting and sorting Scrap Lumber.

Lyle didn't have any money worth speaking of, but Bunny did. Lyle being the smooth talker he was, persuaded Bunny to move to the tree-laden mountains of Montana. Lyle continued to collect Scrap Lumber and because he didn't have to work for a living, he took up chainsaw art to fill his day. Bunny, who had convinced herself that she was younger than she really was, took up downhill skiing. One day when Bunny was skiing down a steep run (she really should have stayed on the bunny hill where she belonged), she lost control and ran into a tree. Bunny died on the spot, and Lyle was left with a tidy sum.

Lyle told the ski lodge owner he wouldn't sue if he could cut down the tree that his wife hit. The ski lodge owner, relieved he wouldn't have to cough up lawyers' fees and go through a trial, gladly agreed and cut down the tree and gave it to him. Lyle took the tree and carved a replica of Bunny downhill skiing. He said he put the carving in his front yard to honor Bunny's memory, but he and everyone else knew it was a clever way for him to show off his art.

One day a young cowgirl named Karen walked into his shop and said, "I love your carving of the old woman skiing. Was that your grandmother?" Lyle didn't know what to say so he just said, "Yes she was my grandmother. We called her Bunny for short." Karen, the young cowgirl, replied, "That's so sweet of you." She hung around for a while and then said to Lyle, "If you will teach me how to carve with a chainsaw, I'll teach you how to rope and ride." He agreed. She literally lassoed him, tied him up with her ropes, and took him for a ride into the sunset.

They ended up in Northern Minnesota on a farm that they found out had been homestead by Ole and Lena Olson. Right after they moved in Karen talked Lyle into building her a large horse stable where she could raise and breed horses. Well, all his money, time and energy was used up on horses and Lyle had no time left for his hobby of collecting Scrap Lumber and creating art with his chainsaw.

One day when Karen, the young cowgirl, was out riding, her horse reared up. She was thrown off and broke her neck. She died doing what she loved. Lyle sold the horses, and used half of the stable for storing his beloved Scrap Lumber, and he turned the other half into a chainsaw art museum.

He never married again, twice was enough. The Olson homestead was finally being used for what Ole originally built it for, i.e., a Scrap Lumber haven. Ole, who had been dead for a long time, could finally rest in peace and Lyle died a happy man.

This is most certainly true.

CHAPTER SIX

HOW THE MEN OF THE DEPRESSION ERA USED SCRAP LUMBER

During the Depression men used
Scrap Lumber one board at a time.

Men of the Depression Era made
sure the Pastor's needs were taken
care of before their own needs.

HOW THE MEN OF THE DEPRESSION ERA USED SCRAP LUMBER

• A man needed Scrap Lumber to shore up a lumber crib that was bursting at the seams.

• Scrap Lumber was used to poke out gunk and/or animals that were stuck in culverts.

• When a leg on a three-legged milking stool gave out and the stool tipped over and the whole pail of milk that Bossie so generously gave ended up all over the barn floor and on the barn clothes, it was time to brace up the stool with a piece of Scrap Lumber.

• Scrap Lumber poles were used to prod Bossie out of the pasture and into the barn when it was time to milk her.

• When the burning barrel got so full that the weight of the ashes made the barrel start to lean like the tower of Pisa in Italy that they never bothered to fix (and now look at the mess they're in), it was shored up with pieces of Scrap Lumber.

• When the seats in the outhouse developed fine-line cracks, men nailed some Scrap Lumber underneath the seat to bring the cracks together because they knew if they didn't, they'd get pinched and there would be more than the dogs that would howl.

• When the wind took the outhouse door off the hinges a piece of Scrap Lumber was just the ticket for a new temporary lock (that usually became the permanent lock.)

• When the outhouse's accessories went from Monkey Wards catalogs to peach papers to toilet paper it was time to make a holder for the real stuff.

• When the North Wind blew his top and ripped the tar paper that was so carefully anchored around the house Scrap Lumber pieces were furiously pounded in to hold the tar paper in place until the house could be banked with hay bales and before the wind switched and started coming out of the West.

• When the drifts were as high as the brooder house and the chores needed to be done and there was no way to get to the barn without sinking up to your knees in snow, Scrap Lumber boards were nailed to the bottom of a man's rubbers and then secured with twine so Bossie could get milked before her bag exploded.

• When the fire needed stoking and the coal bin was on empty Scrap Lumber would save the day.

• When the mud, river, or snow depth needed measuring, a good Scrap Lumber pole was just as reliable as any store bought yard stick.

• If the Mr. or the Mrs. were a little bit too rotund, and the rungs on a ladder couldn't take it any more and snapped, Scrap Lumber broom handles were just the ticket.

• Peg legs for humans or animals were carefully chiseled out of Scrap Lumber and were just as good as factory-made ones.

•When the men were driving around looking at
the fields on Sunday afternoon and they parked
the car in the ditch so they could all go check to
see if wheat rust had developed, most men had
enough common sense to put a good size chunk of
Scrap Lumber in front of the wheels so the car
wouldn't roll so far in the ditch that it would be
stuck clear up to the rusty lug nuts which would
prevent them from getting back in time to eat
supper that the women had made.

•When the car went on the fritz and the underneath had to be checked because she wouldn't turn
over and the Mrs. had to get to church, car ramps
could be quickly fashioned out of hunks and blocks
of wood.

•Rusty old cars and trucks in the grove were
blocked up with Scrap Lumber so mice and skunks
didn't get in and insurance didn't have to be
bought on a vehicle that would never be used
again.

•When the rubber wore off the foot-feed and all
they had was a piece of metal sticking up, they
glued a piece of Scrap Lumber on the foot feed so
it would at least get them through harvest.

•Yearly bushel-to-the-acre facts could be easily
seen and remembered when they were written on
a Scrap Lumber board nailed to the granary wall.

•When the back gave out from age and pulling
Canadian thistles and wild oats, the Mrs. put a
good-sized piece of Scrap Lumber on the bed
spring so her man could be as good as new in the
morning.

• When wagons, outbuildings, back steps, mailboxes, tailgates on pickups, feeding troughs, corncribs, slats on binder canvases or running boards on Model T's needed shoring up, propping up or shimming up, Scrap Lumber was a lifesaver until there was time to do it right — which sometimes never came.

• Hunting shacks and deer stands were standing testimonials to the necessity and importance of having a good-sized Scrap Lumber pile available.

• When, after fourteen years of trying, the big buck was finally downed but taxidermy was too expensive, the antlers were backed with Scrap Lumber and hung in the living room for all the inlaws to see.

• Signs of all sorts were made from Scrap Lumber and displayed on poles, trees or anything else that would secure them. Signs such as: "Barn Dance Here on Saturday night," "Picklers for Sale," "Boat 4 Sale," "Hay for Sale — Round or Square," "Manure Spreader for Sale," "U pik Strawberries," "No Hunting," "No Trespassing," "Keep Out," "Stray Dogs will be Shot," "Dead End," "Modern Housekeeping," and "I will not be Responsible for any of my Wife's Debts".

• When a man needed to show off his new pickup he loaded it up with Scrap Lumber and drove around the countryside and in to town so the rest of the world could see he was a man who had places to go and things to fix.

• When a man retired and moved his house, his Mrs., and his Scrap Lumber pile to town, he had so much time on his hands that he started making Yard Art for the Mrs. to put in her flower gardens, yard, or anywhere else she would put it.

CHAPTER SEVEN

HOW THE WOMEN OF THE DEPRESSION ERA USED SCRAP LUMBER

Women of the Depression Era needed Scrap Lumber for various reasons but their men sure didn't make it easy for them to get their hands on it.

HOW THE WOMEN OF THE DEPRESSION ERA USED SCRAP LUMBER

• When the overalls had fallen off the clothesline on a windy March Monday it was time to brace up the old clothesline pole with some Scrap Lumber. If that didn't work the Mrs. sometimes asked for steel post clotheslines or a new-fangled dryer like Canasta-playing town women used, though she never got them.

• When the handle flew off the rolling pin and the Mrs. was knee deep in flour and lard, she wedged a piece of Scrap Lumber into the end of the pin, and it was good enough until she got so many slivers she said, "Enough's enough."

• The Mrs. propped up hanging branches laden with crab apples that were drooping on the ground so worms, raccoons or any other foragers wouldn't get the apples before she got around to canning them or making apple crisp with dry oatmeal from the "windfalls."

• Gardens proliferated with Scrap Lumber. Two sticks and a string were used to measure out rows. What was growing where was marked on a Scrap Lumber stick on the ends of each planted row. Peonies, sweet peas, tomato plants and anything else that wasn't strong enough to stand on its own were held up by stakes from Scrap Lumber. Scarecrows of Scrap Lumber were made to insure all the hard work of planting and maintaining the garden wasn't in vain.

•Scrap Lumber was given to the church for manger scenes, church supper sandwich boards, homemade benches for Bible School, shoring up pews, tract racks and cemetery signs that read "Keep Off Grass."

•When the river started to rise and the basement was taking on water Scrap Lumber blocks were used to get the deep freeze the Mrs. had gotten as a tenth anniversary present off the floor.

•When the brooder hens were nasty and you needed their eggs, and they weren't about to let you have them, a good Scrap Lumber poking stick let you win.

•Women made "Pullet Eggs for Sale" signs so they could try to accumulate a little egg money from the brooders' nests to create their own nest egg.

•Women nailed a growth sign made of Scrap Lumber to the outside of the brooder house which was used to measure kids who were usually growing about as fast as weeds.

•Out of necessity, and certainly long before shabby chic was in vogue, women made picture frames out of Scrap Lumber barn wood.

•When the old makeshift cupboards in the cellar didn't have doors that stayed shut due to climate change or canning jars of gooseberry or plum sauce that were too wide for the shelves, Scrap Lumber pieces pounded on the doors made secure locks.

• Propping windows open required different lengths of Scrap Lumber sticks depending upon how much air was needed for circulation in a room. The longest sticks were used by women when they were Spring Housecleaning and by kids when they were sneaking cigarettes in the upstairs bedrooms. The shortest sticks were used in the middle of the winter to air it out when all the kids had measles, mumps and chicken pox all at the same time or when the air from the wood stove was so thick you had to thin it out a little, (but not too much, lest heat was wasted.)

• A two-sided sign that read "Occupied" on one side, and "Empty" on the other side, was made to hang on the door of the outhouse. It was used at family reunion picnics when there were so many people in attendance that no one knew who was coming, who was going, or who belonged to whom.

• Hanging Scrap Lumber in the shape of paddles or wooden spoons in conspicuous places around the barn and house kept the kids in line the majority of time. If that didn't work, they were put in use for lickins'.

CHAPTER EIGHT

HOW THE KIDS OF THE DEPRESSION ERA USED SCRAP LUMBER

Scrap Lumber that was "fair game" for Depression Era kids.

HOW THE KIDS OF THE DEPRESSION ERA USED SCRAP LUMBER

• After getting a good lickin' kids tied their essentials in a red or blue farmer's hanky. Then they tied the bandanna to a Scrap Lumber pole, put it over their shoulder, and ran away from home for a couple hours. These hobo sticks were also used at Halloween for a costume accessory.

• Stilts were made of Scrap Lumber to intimidate short kids and to be used just in case one wanted to run away from home and join the circus.

• Toy guns were crudely whittled from Scrap Lumber for playing Cops and Robbers. When kids were too old to play Cops and Robbers they fashioned swords and daggers out of big hunks of Scrap Lumber for King of the Castle games in the hay mound.

• Scrap Lumber poles were used to knock down birds' nests and bee hives that prairie kids pretended were *Piñatas* filled with candy. Even though they had never seen a *Piñata* they had read about them in fourth grade geography class.

• Signs that read "Free Kittens" or "Nectar for Sale" didn't make a kid rich, but it took up time.

• In a pinch Scrap Lumber was used as a bat for kitten ball if a real bat wasn't available, and for bases when they couldn't find the gunny sacks.

• Scrap Lumber was used to make homemade airplanes, kites, go-carts or anything else kids knew they couldn't afford to buy.

• A Scrap Lumber stick was used to draw a line in the sand for a serious, game of "I'll bet my medium-sized steelie for two of your yellow cat-eye marbles."

• Kids, with the help of their parents, fashioned miniature windmills, bookends and birdhouses as woodworking projects for the 4-H County Fair.

• Town kids, who weren't in 4-H but were in Scouts, made little derby cars out of Scrap Lumber so at least they'd learn a little bit about working with wood.

• Kids used Scrap Lumber to build tree houses and slingshots and the mean kids sat in their tree houses and shot anything that walked by that they didn't like.

• Forts, teepee poles and playhouses in the woods (complete with orange crate cupboards) were all built compliments of Scrap Lumber.

• Homemade Scrap Lumber croquet mallets were used not only for croquet, but for hitting pocket gophers over the head.

• Flipping roadkill full of maggots off the road and into the ditches required a long piece of Scrap Lumber.

• Booster pedals for bikes and trikes were made from blocks of Scrap Lumber for kids who were a little too short.

• Swings in trees and teeter-totters in backyards were fashioned from Scrap Lumber so country kids could have the perks of a town kid, a city park right in their own farmyards.

• Little boys pretended they were Huckleberry Finn by maneuvering Scrap Lumber rafts up and down ditches that were full of runoff.

• Little girls made crosses out of Scrap Lumber to mark the spots where they had buried their kittens.

• Teenage boys loaded up Scrap Lumber on stoneboats and took it to town to make a bonfire for homecoming festivities.

CHAPTER NINE

WHY MEN SAY THEY SAVE SCRAP LUMBER

Men say they save Scrap Lumber
because you never know when there's
going to be another Depression.

WHY MEN SAY THEY SAVE SCRAP LUMBER

Men say they save Scrap Lumber because:

. . . you just never know when you need a hunk.

. . . they paid good money for it.

. . . it's just too good to throw away.

. . . there might be another Depression.

. . . a guy could use it to barter.

. . . it's too good to burn.

. . . how else would you fill up a garage.

. . . it doesn't cost anything.

. . . a guy can dream about building a cabin with it.

. . . they don't collect and save buttons, fabric, figurines, dolls, snow villages, anniversary napkins, bread twisties, margarine tubs or Engelbert Humperdinck concert ticket stubs.

CHAPTER TEN

WHY WOMEN SAY MEN SAVE SCRAP LUMBER

Women say men save Scrap Lumber
because they want to be like Norm.

WHY WOMEN SAY MEN SAVE SCRAP LUMBER

Women say MEN save Scrap Lumber because:

... of a hormone imbalance.

... it's just a man thing.

... it's a status thing, you know, like King on the Hill.

... it gives them something to haul in their pickups.

... they don't know any better.

... they can fantasize they're just like Norm.

... it's their way of getting even.

... it's a blood disease.

... their dad did, their grandpa did, their great-grandpa did, etc.

... it gives them an excuse to buy a chainsaw.

CHAPTER ELEVEN

THE TOP TEN WAYS A MAN CAN KEEP BOTH HIS SCRAP LUMBER PILE AND HIS HAPPY HOME

Note to men: Learn to hide your lumber like women hide bags of trinkets, clothes, etc...

THE TOP TEN WAYS A MAN CAN KEEP BOTH HIS SCRAP LUMBER PILE AND HIS HAPPY HOME

(1) Learn how to vacuum, clean toilets and iron. Then do it! The Mrs. will be so content she'll forget to nag you about your Scrap Lumber heap.

(2) Buy a pickup that's so rusty and dilapidated the Mrs. won't want to drive it or try to clean it up. Store and haul your Scrap Lumber in the back of it. To make doubly sure your Scrap Lumber is protected from the weather and the wife, equip your pickup with a padlocked topper. Store the padlock key in your cowboy boots.

(3) If you go to an auction and buy a heap of Scrap Lumber and can't figure out where to put it or how you're going to tell the Mrs., just do what she does- hide it for a while. When she goes shopping she's smart enough to hide a few bags of goodies she bought to bring out at a later date. When you ask her, "Is that new?" and she says, "You mean this old thing?" know that she isn't lying to you. Dimes to dollars it's been in a bag that's been hidden in a closet or under the bed for a long time.

(4) Every once in a while surprise the Mrs. by fixing up a busted leg on an old table. Let her know it was a good thing you had a Scrap Lumber pile so it didn't cost anything to fix it up.

(5) If you keep all your Scrap Lumber in one place you're only asking for trouble. Store some in the basement, some in the garage, some in the attic of the garage, some behind the garage, some on the left side of the garage, some on the right side of the garage, some in the back of the garage, and some in the back of your pickup that's in the garage. That way it won't look like such a big pile.

(6) Tell the Mrs. that most of the Scrap Lumber came from the fallen trees on your grandfather's farm and now that he's dead it's the only thing you have to remember him by.

(7) When the Mrs. threatens to get rid of your Scrap Lumber pile convince her that there could be another Depression and at least you could use it to make toys for the kids at Christmas. Also, inform her there isn't an infinite amount of fuel available and she should be thankful that you are looking after her and the family's welfare by having the foresight to save a Scrap Lumber heap to burn just in case it would be needed.

(8) Open up one of your handyman's workshop magazine to an article on "Surprising the Mrs. with a Beautiful Jewelry Box Made with Your Own Hands Using only Scrap Lumber." Place the article on top of the Scrap Lumber pile so it's visible to the Mrs. just in case she happens to walk by the pile with thoughts of throwing some hunks away.

(9) If the Mrs. is the type that sorts dust and alphabetizes spices, you have no choice but to sort your Scrap Lumber. Separate the pine from the walnut from the good oak pieces into separate piles. Then, separate them by length, width and breadth. Next separate them by the number of knots on each piece. Label each piece with a sticky

note explaining where it came from and how you're going to use it. Stack it neatly making sure there are no dust clumps or cobwebs on any of the pieces. Wrap each piece in Saran Wrap and cover the neatly stacked pile with a tarp that you've duct-taped around the whole pile. Label it, "Scrap Lumber: I plan to use it up shortly."

(10) If worse comes to worse and the Mrs. gives you an ultimatum like it's either her or the Scrap Lumber, call up a buddy who lives on an old farm and rent space in an old shed or barn from him. That way you can keep your happy home and your Scrap Lumber pile, too.

CHAPTER TWELVE

"CLOSE ENOUGH" COUNTS IN HORSESHOES AND IN MEASURING SCRAP LUMBER OR WHY WOMEN ARE FROM EARTH AND MEN ARE FROM OUTER SPACE

Need we say anymore?

Maybe it's because
he played with
Lincoln Logs and
Tinker Toys.

CLOSE ENOUGH COUNTS IN HORSESHOES AND IN MEASURING SCRAP LUMBER, OR WHY MEN ARE FROM OUTER SPACE AND WOMEN ARE FROM EARTH

Traditionally it is men, the male species, who collect and store Scrap Lumber. It is women, the female species, who put up with these heaps of Scrap Lumber until they can't stand the helter-skelter mess any longer and give the ultimatum, "Get some order to your crap Scrap Lumber heaps or choose between me or them!" This is a given, and here are the circumstances.

Men are not known for their ability to organize important thoughts in their head or to grasp the significance of details. For example, ask Darrell Odegaard when his anniversary is, when his first child was born, when the license plate fees are due on his pickup, when his wife's birthday is, what his mother's middle name is or what year his little sister graduated from high school and the response is something like, "Oh ya, about . . ." or "Whatever," or ". . .Close 'nuff."

His anniversary is about spring planting time, his first child was born before his second one, his license plate fees are due when his wife pays them, her birthday is something she quit celebrating so why should he remember it, his mother's middle name isn't important because everyone just calls her Grandma anyway, and his little sister graduated sometime after he did. Ask him to be more specific on any of these and he'll just shrug his shoulders and say, ". . . close 'nuff."

Ask these same questions of his wife, Carol, and one learns that their anniversary is March 19th, and they were married at 7:00 p.m. with the "I now pronounce you . . . stuff" said at exactly 7:42 p.m. in 1953 at Polk County, MN and there were 422 people in attendance, a lunch was served in the church basement, there was no wedding kiss, no dance, the cake was made by Mrs. Ethel Lang, and the bridesmaids' dresses were a frosty, pale yellow with wide hems, . . .

Their first child was little Christopher and he was born right on his due date even though he was the first baby and should have been late. The date was February 22, 1956, and the place was Trinity Hospital in Grand Forks, ND. Labor had lasted 14 hours, a little ether was given to ease the pain, and the attending physician was Dr. Hyram Clarke because the real doctor was at a conference in Williston. His weight was 8 lbs. and 15 oz. and if he could have held on another day or so he might have topped his first cousin who lived on a farm and still only weighed in at 9 lbs. even. Christopher's first visitors were Agnes the Nurse and Grandma Tollekson who just happened to have scheduled her cataract appointment in Grand Forks for that day even though her real eye doctor in Fergus Falls was available and she couldn't see the baby clearly anyway because of the "drops." His first toy was a yellow, plastic rattle in the shape of a clown's head from the Ruth Circle that had been packed in the overnight bag since December "just in case, . . ."

His license plates expire in March as they always have and always will because he never buys a
new pickup. He never washes his pickup because if
the cop can't read the license plate number he'll
never get pinched.

Carol says her birthday is October 31 and it
shouldn't be so hard for him to remember because
half the time he thinks she's a witch, and she
doesn't really mind him knowing how old she is
because he'll always be three years older. He
should know that forgetting her birthday is something she wants her friends to do, but that she still
wants him to remember it with a nice present just
for her, not for the kitchen, and just because he
gives her a gift he doesn't have to make a big deal
of it and remind everyone that she is older, but, by
golly, dinner out at Pete's Place for walleye would
be nice, but how many hints does she have to drop,
and what if they were sitting there eating on a
weeknight and someone they knew saw them. What
would they say they were celebrating? Halloween
without a costume on? Shoot, if he can figure out
how many tanks of anhydrous ammonia he needs
for the bean fields, can't he figure out a good excuse
for a night out with his wife?

His mother's middle name? Someday after she is
gone he'll have to know this to get a Visa Card.
How can someone be too uncaring to remember his
mother's middle name? That shouldn't be too hard,
and it's certainly less complicated than memorizing
his military ID number which he'll remember until
his dying day. Can't he even guess her middle name
just might be Carol, the same as his wife's first
name? Oh well, what do you expect from someone
who hauls a load of Scrap Lumber around in the
back of his pickup for six years without using one
piece and then transfers it all to a new pile along-

side the garage and starts another pile in the back of the now empty bed of the pickup?

And his little sister's graduation? Now, why can't a guy cipher or reckon numbers? If she is ten years younger than he is, and he graduated in 1953 and neither of them flunked or got moved ahead, isn't it as clear as glass that she would have graduated in 1963? What is this about men and things being "close 'nuff?" Heavens to Betsy, life isn't a big game of horseshoes. Sometimes "close" just isn't enough. East is east and West is west and ten is ten and five is five and red is red! This background knowledge on the species, then, logically brings one to the topic of Scrap Lumber measurements.

Most lumber is purchased by men, and about 33% of this lumber becomes Scrap Lumber. For some reason, "close 'nuff" counts for men in lumber just as it does with dates, ages, weights, etc. For example, a 1" x 10" rough-cut board might be 3/4" x 9 1/4", or maybe 1 1/2" x 10", but the actual width isn't important because no matter how wide it is, it will be called "a one-by."

The good news is that if two 2" x 4s" come from the same load they might have the same dimensions. However, if they don't come from the exact same stack, one might be 1 3/4" x 3 3/4", and the other 2" x 4 1/4". Close enough. Similarly a 2" x 4" board that is 6' long just might by 1 1/2" by 3 1/2" but so what? It will be 6' long and that's for sure. Now, of course, whatever is being built will be uneven so the Mr. goes to the handy, dandy Scrap Lumber pile to find the exact size of Scrap Lumber to act as a shim to even things out.

The bad news, as all women know, is he won't

find whatever size he needs so he will have to go to the lumber yard to buy a piece of board of the exact size to act as a shim to even out the difference in the width of the two boards which were the same size, but really aren't, and as long as he has made the trip to town, he might as well get more than he needs just in case he doesn't get enough.

When he gets home he throws the excess in the Scrap Lumber pile for the next time when he needs a little piece of that same width, but he won't be able to find it because by then it will be buried by more Scrap Lumber and to save time it will be just as easy to go to town to get new lumber to shim up the other pieces that are the same size, but really aren't.

Similarly, you can buy a "cord" of wood, but the size of a cord, which should be 4" x 4" x 8" or 128 cubic feet, can differ greatly. A stack of 2" x 4s" that are 6' long will still be called a "cord" by most men regardless of the height of the pile, and this stack will then be priced unaccordingly.

When you get right down to brass tacks, it really doesn't matter because this wood will be held together with nails which are bought by the pound, although they are rarely weighed. A handful of some size nails is a pound, and two handfuls of the same size nail at the next store is a pound, and it doesn't seem to matter whose hands are measuring the nails. Like lumber, 16 ounces or a pound of nails might only weigh 14 ounces. Furthermore, ten-penny nails do not cost a dime, and they aren't made of pennies, but no one seems to care.

Most lumber is bought by guys who think a Perfect Ten is 36-24-36, and this is where the problem originates. So when women try to analyze men and their understanding of measurements, they realize men are a little bit foggy about numbers and details.

On the other hand, when a woman has a recipe that calls for "lard the size of an egg" she knows exactly what size the egg referred to is, and the recipe turns out perfectly. When a recipe calls for a "fistful of oatmeal" she knows without question that the fist will be the size of Mrs. Lars Groven's fist, and not the size of the fist of the County Public Health Nurse who pulled lice out of school children's hair.

Like Fanny Odegaard said in 1962 when she tried to squeeze into her first pair of panty-hose, "Well, you can just tell that these things were designed by men. Who else would figure you can put a 44" waist into a 14" tube?"

This is most certainly true.

CHAPTER THIRTEEN

THE ART OF STACKING SCRAP LUMBER

A Type O Scrap Lumber Stacker will
drive most women over the brink.

NEW FINISHED
NEW PLYWOOD SCRAPS
NEW FIBER BOARD
NEW ROUGH CUT
USED FINISHED
USED PLYWOOD SCRAPS
USED FIBER BOARD
USED ROUGH CUT
USED BARE
USED STAINED
USED PAINTED

TEAK
MAHOGANY
WALNUT
CHERRY MAPLE
BIRCH or OAK
WHITE PINE
KNOTTY PINE
CHEAP, WARPED PINE
BALSAM
TWISTED ASPEN 2X4's

THE ART OF STACKING
SCRAP LUMBER

There are as many ways to stack Scrap Lumber as there are men in the world. In other words, there are four: Type A, Type B, Type O and Type R.

Types A and B follow their proclaimed psychological profiles. Type O stands for Ordinary and when he brings home more Scrap Lumber his wife says things like, "O, Heavens to Betsy!" Type R is short, of course, for Rich.

It is easiest to analyze Type R. Along with Rich, Type R can also stand for Rare because Rich husbands are of the rarest breed. Type R's do not stack Scrap Lumber. They handle it in short order. They stand in their brick-paved driveways, leaning against their dark green Land Rovers in their L. L. Bean pants and Pendleton sweaters and call their brothers-in-law on the cell phone and say, "Hey, Bud. Forrest here. Sure, sure, everything's fine. Good to be back from the Riviera. Just wonderin' if you could use some leftover mahogany from the new staircase, or if I should hire someone to haul it to the landfill?"

Type R's never have a Scrap Lumber pile, a Scrap Iron pile, a sawdust pile, extra tires or grease circles on their garage floors. They only accumulate paper: stocks, bonds, deeds and legal documents. Their yards and garages are as neat as a pin, and they do not have to lift more than their cell phones to keep them that way. Ironically, the wives of a

Type R stacker wouldn't notice if their husbands had a Scrap Lumber pile because it is dark when they get home from bridge group and just getting light out when they leave for the golf course. Wives of Type R men see their husbands about as often as they see their yards and garages in the daylight.

The next easiest type to analyze is Type A because they, too, are pretty rare. Type A Scrap Lumber stackers are true to the psychological profiles of Type A personalities. They are organized, detailed perfectionists who work to see both the forest and the trees. When they miss either, they can't cope and end up having a quadruple bypass.

Type A stackers sort their Scrap Lumber piles at least four times a year. They begin with two main piles according to size. Within each category are lesser sorts: used or new, painted and stained or bare, and rough-cut or finished. For example, Hank Bark puts pieces longer than 3' (dock-repair size) in one pile, and shorter pieces in another. At the bottom of each pile he has meticulously placed longer Scrap Lumber or planks crosswise to hold the Scrap piles above the ground or garage floor so they won't get wet. Stickler for details that he is, he, of course, puts the used Scrap Lumber at the bottom of each pile lining up the ends and leaving a little air space between the boards.

Within these lesser sorts of new or used are divisions according to type. Above the used boards are the rough-cut ones followed by the finished ones.

Within each type (used, rough-cut, finished), he sorts according to kind with the cheapest used lumber on the bottom, the next cheapest used boards above that, and on up to the most expensive used lumber. Then he begins the rough-cut sort with the cheapest on the bottom of the rough-cut section, but above the most expensive used Scrap Lumber. Again it goes up through the "food chain" to the most expensive rough-cut before he begins stacking the cheapest finished boards. This is all one pile with three basic divisions and any number of subsets in each of the three.

This same system is applied to the pile with shorter-than-three-feet boards. (A lucky 4-H kid will find mahogany finished boards at the top of the short Scrap Lumber pile. This is guaranteed at least a "blue," if not a Grand Champion in the birdhouse entries at the County Fair in August.)

In between the four annual sortings, these men sweep off the piles monthly, realign the ends of the piles weekly, and pat the top boards daily. Every trip past the pile elicits a low whistle and proud smile. Type A stackers forgo quail and grouse hunting and spend most of September and October brushing boxelder bugs off their precious lumber piles.

Academics who have received grant money from Democrats at the federal level feel that these piles and sorts are Type A stackers' attempts to reconstruct life according to the biological systemic arrangement of Kingdom, Phylum, Subphylum, Class, Order, Family, Genus and Species. (No one has ever read their reports, because no one reads academic papers any more preferring to watch pro-wrestling for enlightenment.)

Interestingly though, the Loopy Ladies Home Study Club in Lyngdal Township also studied this matter and really hit the nail on the head. Their research, completed in two year's less time and at no expense, showed that the Type A Stacking System had been borrowed from Detroit. Quite simply, the original two piles based on Length equated to sedan or pickup. The Type, (used, rough-cut, etc.) was a carry over of Brand such as Chevy, Pontiac or Buick. The next sort, based on Kind, had to do with Model such as Bel-Air, Chieftain or Skylark.

So just as one could have a rough-cut 2" x 4" pine board that was 2' long, one could also have a slightly used Dodge Dart in the shed. In another part of the shed he might have a finished 1" x 2" cherry board that was 5' long, and he could also have a new Dodge Ram pickup.

Type A stackers generally marry Type B women, but after a few years of marriage these women are hard to define. Because they have married Type A men, these Type B women — who entered the world and their marriages with some common sense — throw up their hands and let their husbands take over all responsibilities because anything they do isn't quite right. However, all is not lost for these women. With no responsibilities they are free to read movie magazines, watch cable shows about the rich and famous Type R spouses, and polish their toe nails in the latest colors. After a few years these women can't even remember their ages.

If a Type A stacker — who marries for love and momentarily forgets about control— marries a Type A woman who also sorts dust and wants control, there is more than Scrap Lumber to worry about. Ninety-three percent of Scrap Lumber stacker divorces are between Type A men who have married Type A women. Just like Tillie Olson trying to wiggle into her wedding girdle for her

Silver Doings, Type A and Type A just can't get it on!

The third most common type of stacker is the Type B male. Type B personalities stack and sort, but they don't fret or get bent out of shape like a Scrap Lumber board does when it's accidentally left out in the elements too long. Their Scrap Lumber piles usually get sorted when the B types can't see the forest for the trees. But, if other things come up and they don't get around to sorting for a while, that's okay with them, too. They always get it done, but without developing clotted up arteries from worrying about their Scrap Lumber. Their Scrap Lumber messes are usually manageable, and if they aren't, these men don't notice.

If a Type B sorter is married to a Type A woman he usually spends his time in the garage or basement so he doesn't have to listen to his Type A woman rant and rave. If she really gets on her high horse, a Type B stacker jumps in his pickup and drives around until he feels enough time has gone by for her to settle down.

Type B stackers who are marred to Type B women have the most successful marriages because both of the type B's are free to sort and clean in their own due time. The B may just be short for Bliss.

There have been no major research projects of the Type B stackers because the Republicans used up the grant money for oil exploration. Gladys Borgrud, a Type A farmer's wife from MIlbank, SD who isn't particularly interested in research, oil, defense or politics, saw through the whole issue in '54 when, upon hearing her daughter, Arlys, announce that she was marrying the Thorstad boy, said, "For Heavens Sake! Someone's gotta get a grip. Who in the world will make the decisions? Two dreamers in one house starving to death because they can't find a drop of milk in their wild imaginations!" Gladys really hit the nail on the head.

Most women are married to Type O. Type O men spring up like Aspen and Burdock. They are everywhere and, like Aspen and Burdock, it is hard to find a good use for them. (Burdock, of course, isn't a kind of lumber. It is more of a Scrap Lumber Wanna-be. It just shows up all over and self-propagates without paying any attention to location. Sort of like a hoodlum from the other side of the tracks.)

The majority of men who save Scrap Lumber are Type O for Ordinary. In one way they are like Type R men because Type O men do not stack Scrap Lumber either, but unlike Type R, they sure save it!

Type O's don't put much thought into how they can use Scrap Lumber. They just collect it. Most Type O stackers had parents who suffered through the Depression. "Use it up, Wear it out, If you haven't got, Do without."

Type O men have had some of the same Scrap Lumber for over forty years but when the Mrs. asks him to get rid of some of it, he just says, "You never know when this will come in handy." She, of course, is thinking, "O for Pete's Sake!" (His name is Leonard, not Pete.) Type O men also save — but do not sort— Scrap Iron, Scrap Tires, nuts, bolts or screws.

A Type O men can't get enough! He buys Scrap Lumber at auctions and when he comes home with another worthless load his dear wife can only utter, "O, for cryin' out loud!" He innocently visits the neighboring farm for coffee and to check on the crops and comes home toting more Scrap Lumber from his Type A neighbor who had a few pieces that stuck out to far defying the Type A System. Well, when Ole brings home 12-footers with nails sticking through them, his wife can only say, "O Lord, What next?" Next, of course, is when he volunteers to help reroof the outhouses at New Hemsedal Lutheran and comes home with, literally, crap. His wife can only shake her head and whisper, "O for Cryin' in the Beer! If God would have wanted us to have more Scrap Lumber, He'd have put a big pile of it right in front of the barn."

Used to cruising through life without a clue, Ole begins another Scrap Lumber pile right in front of the barn just as his unsuspecting wife has suggested. Unlike Type A stacks, this pile has no rhyme or reason to it. It is just a hodgepodge, random collection kind of like the Type O male. His wife, who doesn't notice the new pile until 45 minutes before she expects the first Ladies Aid members to show up, just glares at it as she whips off her everyday apron and moans, "O for stupid!" She doesn't have time to dust it or straighten it or plant trees or hollyhocks in front of it. Out of desperation she jumps in the '56 Ford grain truck and parks it smack in front of the pile and mumbles, "O, Dear Me!," and heads for the house to get her good bone china coffee cups out. All of her "O" phrases translate directly to "What will the neighbors say?"

Type O couples struggle throughout life. It is good that their women belong to Ladies Aid and other women's groups so they don't have to deal.

This is most certainly true.

Pictorial instructions for stacking
Scrap Lumber outside.

Wrong way.

Right way.

CHAPTER FOURTEEN

THE FUTURE OF SCRAP LUMBER PILES: HOW SCRAP LUMBER COULD EVOLVE AND PROLIFERATE

Scrap Lumber multiplies so fast
it can even choke out weeds.

FUTURE OF SCRAP LUMBER: HOW SCRAP LUMBER COULD EVOLVE AND PROLIFERATE

(Note: This story might not be true, but it isn't so far fetched. Just think about it, then.)

It was the latter part of March. The dirty snow piles had melted, the sidewalks were finally cleared of ice, and Betty Busybody was thankful she could at last walk around town without worrying about falling down and breaking a hip. And walk she did. Up one street and down the other, stopping frequently to peer and stare at everyone's houses and yards. It had always been her favorite pastime. After she had finished walking the sidewalks, she started down the alleys.

"Man, oh man. I can't ever remember seeing this many piles of Scrap Lumber," she said to herself as she surveyed the sides and backs of all the garages in all the alleys in town. She got so busy looking and thinking about all the Scrap Lumber heaps that she didn't notice a makeshift skateboard ramp that was sitting smack dab in the middle of an alley. She stumbled over it, grabbed the side of a garage to catch herself from falling, and said out loud, "That's it!" She brushed herself off and headed downtown to City Hall.

She had been a regular there for years. She told Harriet, the no-nonsense, stout City Desk Clerk who was obviously suffering from hotflashes, that she had come to register a complaint. Harriet, who was wiping her face and neck with a hanky that was as big as a diaper, didn't even look up from her computer as she said to Betty, "Is it a different complaint from last week?" "Brand new," Betty said, "and a needed one at that." Harriet handed her a form to fill out, a form Betty had filled out many times. Betty finished, handed it back to Harriet, and said, "Give this to Mayor Magnuson. I'm going to be at City Council Meeting tomorrow night and I want this put on the agenda." Once again Harriet didn't look up as she took the form from Betty. "Make sure you tell him I'll be there," Betty said as she started to leave. Harriet, who was usually slow to anger and the type who bit her tongue, became obviously irked and said, "Maybe you should run for City Council. You're there every month anyway." Betty mumbled back, "Maybe I will someday," even though deep down she and Harriet both knew it was a lie.

As promised Betty Busybody showed up the next night at the City Council Meeting. She started to complain that the town looked like a tornado had hit it with all the Scrap Lumber piles laying around. "Scrap Lumber piles are nothing but a breeding ground for juvenile delinquents, mosquitoes, domestic disturbances, well I could go on and on," she said as everyone on the City Council was praying she wouldn't. "I want to have a law enacted on the books that makes it illegal for anyone to have a Scrap Lumber pile. I don't think that's too much to ask because I just about broke my hip this morning tripping over a heap right in the middle of the alley. Juvenile delinquents, I tell you. And do you think for one minute they'd care if I broke my hip?" The Mayor didn't respond to her concerns or question, but thanked her for her input and told her that the issue would be tabled that night and that they would call a Town Meeting next week so everyone could discuss the issue. She left, and the Mayor and City Council Members, as usual, shook their heads.

Well, the story was just beginning. The town folks got wind of Betty's latest meddling shenanigans through the local newspaper, the local radio stations, the local coffee shops and from Harriet at City Hall. Everyone had an opinion and reacted by attending the Town Meeting to discuss Scrap Lumber. That is, everybody except Betty. She never showed up for Town Meetings when the main topic was a hot issue she'd created. "She can't take the heat. She just generates it," Harriet, the City Desk Clerk, always told everyone.

As the Mayor, Betty and everyone else knew, an overflow, standing-room-only crowd shows up for a Town Meeting. As usual with any hot topic, tempers flair and everyone is trying to talk at once. Mayor Magnuson pounded the gavel and said that the public either had to talk one at a time or no one would be allowed to talk at all. He told them to line up in back of the microphone and warned them that each one only had a couple minutes to make their perspective points. Gracia Green, (her given name was Gracia Brown but she legally changed her name to make a political statement) of the Green Party was the first one at the microphone.

Her green-haired tree-hugging, tree-sitting, nose-pierced, tongue-pierced, "Save the Earth"-tattooed support group stood behind her with posters and signs made from recycled cardboard. She informed the Mayor, the Council, and everyone else in attendance that no one was going to even be able to breathe if people kept cutting down trees, and if people weren't always mutilating trees for nonessential purposes, there would no Scrap

Lumber piles created and thus no reason for this meeting.

Mayor Magnuson politely told her that those in her group who were only wearing leaves and branches for clothes had to leave. He said, "I'm sorry. No shirt, no shoes, no service. That's it." Gracia Green informed him it was a free country and they would not only demand an environmental impact statement, but that they would be back, wearing whatever they wanted to wear. Some townsfolk's booed her.

Bud, the Bearded Local, who was wearing a dirty white teeshirt, wranglers that were too small, and a big wide frayed belt, yelled, "Hey, yous guys, you better stay out of my trees, or I'll get my chainsaw out and then I'll see how fast you can scamper." A couple in the audience snickered. Olga Olson whispered (but everybody heard) to Esther Larson, "Ish, they all need a bath." Mayor Magnuson pounded his gavel, then halfheartedly thanked Gracia Green for her input, and informed her that time was up. He instructed her and her people to sit down.

Next Harley Davidson, wearing a sleeveless black leather vest and, like the Green delegation, sporting a few tattoos — although a different variety of tattoos — got up, cleared his throat and said, "First you tell me and my buddies we can't assemble in my yard. Now my Scrap Lumber, what's next? The girlfriend? My bike?" He looked around the room. His eyes got smaller and darker as he said, "I dare anyone to try get my Scrap Lumber. That's alls I got to say." He rattled a thick silver chain that he held in his hand, looked around and sat down. No one clapped, but everyone appeared to be a little bit more tense.

Serina Severson, or Serina Screwloose, as everyone called this woman who shared her house with 24 cats, 8 dogs, and her bedridden sister, was up next. She pointed to everyone in the audience and said, "Why are you so worried about some Scrap Lumber piles that never hurt anyone when there's all this abortion going on right under our nose, and some say it's right here in town too. That's what I'm hear to talk about." Mayor Magnuson informed her that the issue was Scrap Lumber and not abortion. He told her to sit down. She yelled, "You just wait, all of you. You're going to burn in hell. Every last one of you." She continued yelling until Mayor Magnuson had the local cop, Art Schmidt, escort her out of the building.

Ninety-five-year-old Sven Nordquist spoke next. Holding onto the back of his chair while he was shaking his cane at the audience, he said, "I might as well curl up and die if you're going to take my whittling pile away. What else is there for me to do but whittle and sort? My wife's gone, the dog died, the taxes keep going up, and I'm on a fixed income. Now you want a new school to boot, and kids can't even read." Some one in the audience yelled for Sven to turn down his hearing aid. He stopped, turned it down and continued, "I tell you this, if I don't die soon, I have half a notion to move back to Sweden where I would have the freedom to whittle all year long." He paused, and then continued, "When I came over here, I was told this was the land of the free and the brave. I lived through the Depression, where we didn't throw anything away. I fought in the trenches in the Big One and we didn't back down. I kept my nose to the grindstone and worked hard for a living, and then now I have to sit and defend myself from all this foolishness that someone is dreaming up." Sven was shaking as he sat down. But he had made his point well because all the old timers cheered him on.

Penelope and her people from PETA came to speak their minds too. Many of them were carrying cats, dogs, gerbils and other unidentifiable rodents. Penelope was holding onto her German Shepherd/Wolf dog that was nervously trying to break away from his leash while she was speaking. "We from PETA want a ban on Scrap Lumber piles immediately," she confidently said. "Many of our fine furry friends are trapped in these piles, and end up dying a horrible death. We will hold you all responsible. . .". She was trying to continue but was interrupted by Bud, the Bearded Local, who yelled, "Ya, and if your mutt and any of those other poor excuses for pets that are hanging around here happens to step foot on my property, they're minced meat, and I ain't mincing words!" Mayor Magnuson pounded his gavel and informed Bud that he couldn't talk out of turn. He told Penelope that her time was up, and animals weren't allowed in City Hall. As Penelope and her group got up to leave, she turned and yelled, "Our pets in this room are better behaved than most of the people here." "Ya, right," Bud, the Bearded Local, yelled. "You and all your freak friends can go join the circus." Mayor Magnuson pounded his gavel twice. Olga Olson whispered to Esther Larson in a loud voice, "Ya, No. Where in the world do some of these people come from anyway?"

As usual, ying follows yang, and Buck Huntstad, the President of the Local Chapter of the Hunters Unite or Die Association stood up and said, "All I got to say is this is. The USA and the Declaration of Independence gives us a right to own guns and to hunt." "You mean the Constitution," Sven Nordquist audibly corrected him. "Whatever," said Buck, "and if you read dem gun magazines at all, you know it's written down someplace that it's the law we can own guns and hunt, and you ain't going to take our guns away from us." "What's your point?" one of the Greens yelled. Buck shouted back, "I'm getting to it if you'd just shut up. You had your turn and you didn't make any sense."

Mayor Magnuson pounded his gavel and told Buck he was soon running out of time. Buck started talking faster. "I'm sure everyone knows we have the NRA behind us and they don't mess around with small change. Our group builds deer stands and we use a lot of Scrap Lumber in them deer stands, and if you take our Scrap Lumber away . . .".

One of the Greens who was wearing twigs and leaves for clothes yelled, "Makes a lot of sense! Mutilating our beloved trees with deer stands, doesn't it?" "Buck glared at the Green who was wearing twigs and leaves, sneered at him and then said, "Where did those leaves and twigs that you're wearing come from? Looks like you've mutilated a few trees yourself." "That's right, you tell' um Buck," Bud, the Bearded Local, yelled. Mayor Magnuson pounded his gavel three times, called for a break and got up and went to his office to have a cool one. All the City Council Members (who hadn't said a word up to this point) joined him. So did Art Schmidt, the local sheriff. When they returned to start up the meeting again, no one had left except for Serina who had been hauled out by Sheriff Art Schmidt and some of the PETA folks along with their pets.

When the Mayor and his City Council Members returned, he told the overflow audience that there was only time for three more opinions. Ben Bauer was next. He had been standing through the whole break to make sure his voice would be heard. "I've been farming in this area for thirty years. My father and grandfather farmed the same land before me, and my great-grandfather homesteaded it. They came from Germany with nothing, and built it up with their own sweat and tears so I could continue farming." His voice, which sounded like the drone of a dull John Deere, put some of the old timers to sleep. Sven Nordquist, with his head back and his mouth opened wide, was snoring audibly. It was 8:45 p.m. and way past Sven's bedtime.

Ben continued, "I know sometimes things can become eyesores, and maybe I shouldn't talk because I've got so much old machinery rusting out in the grove it's a sight to behold. But I've been on the tractor planting all week, and I've had lots of time to think and I think I came up with a good solution." More oldtimers yawned, but others started to perk up. Sven emitted a loud double snort and woke himself up. He opened his eyes and his head became erect. Ben continued, "I've been thinking it's impossible to get rid of all the Scrap Lumber piles, but maybe we only need to get rid of the piles that are really eyesores."

He looked at Sheriff Art Schmidt and said, "Maybe you could get those prisoners out working to help us clean up the bad piles. I hear all they do is watch colored TV and lay around shooting baskets anyway. You know, it makes me mad. We're wasting all of our taxpayers money on them when the rest of us have worked for generations." As he continued his voice became more agitated and all of the oldtimers, including Sven, were now wide awake and taking in every word. "Sometimes I get so mad thinking about it I could just spit," he said as he cleared a hunk out of his throat and into his farmer's hanky that he pulled out of the side pocket of his bib overalls. Bud joined in again, "I hear they even get turkey and all the trimmings for Thanksgiving. I think you should give them roadkill." Mayor Magnuson pounded the gavel four times and warned Bud, the Bearded Local, that if he heard one more outburst from him, he'd be out. Both Bud and Ben sat down.

Herbert Grossman was next and he didn't waste any time. He said to the sheriff, "I have to agree with Ben but while you're at it, maybe some of them welfare women and all their illegitimate kids could help too. I'd like to be on the dole too, but I guess some of us have more pride." Ben nodded and many people clapped at his suggestion. Bud, the Bearded Local, clapped the loudest and continued clapping until Mayor Magnuson pounded the gavel five times.

Clara Barton, the school nurse, was the last to speak. She methodically turned her head in every direction, took a deep breath, looked at the Mayor, the City Council Members and the audience, and began, "I'm not familiar with all the Scrap Lumber piles around town, but I'm real familiar with the Scrap Lumber pile that's sitting behind the school. You know school grounds are public property. It's really essential that we get rid of it because I spend half my day pulling slivers out of kids' hands. Plus, it's dangerous. Someone could get crawl under that pile and suffocate or step on a rusty nail that's sticking up and get tetanus, or get sick chewing on the pieces that have been treated with arsenic or creosote. Those are the issues that concern me," she said as she straightened her skirt before she sat down. "Serves them right if they're that stupid," Bud, the Bearded Local, yelled. Mayor Magnuson pounded his gavel six times and told Bud to hit the road. Bud left but not before saying, "Remember yous guys, you freaks, I'm warning you. No trespassing on my property!"

Finally after two and a half hours of wrangling

Mayor Magnuson pounded the gavel seven times and said they'd take all suggestions into consideration and vote on it at the next City Council Meeting. He thanked everyone for coming. Everyone left the meeting at once and gathered in their little groups with their spokesperson out by their cars and pickups to plan the next strategy.

The next week headlines in the local newspaper were all about the heated Town Meeting. The photographer of the local newspaper had taken several pictures at the meeting and they were all in the local newspaper. He even had taken a picture of the Scrap Lumber pile outside the school, put it in the paper, and titled it, "Are Our Kids Safe?"

Lo and behold, the next week — which was two weeks before the next City Council Meeting — a paid ad appeared in the local newspaper. It read: *If you, one of your children, or any acquaintances have gotten a sliver, bruise mark, tetanus shot or stomachache from chewing on the Scrap Lumber piles at school, or have been injured physically or emotionally in any other way by the pile, please call Jack Shyster at: 1-800-Gotchya Law Firm.*

Everyone read the paper and looked at the many pictures. Most scanned the paid ad, and sure as shootin', a few responded. Betty Busybody was the first to call. She always called 800 numbers because they were free. She told Jack Shyster at the 1-800-Gotchya Law Firm that she didn't have a sliver, but had just about broken a hip on a makeshift skateboard ramp in the alley. Jack Shyster told her it would pay for her to come down for a consultation because they would be able to help her. He explained that she could develop what is termed "emotional arthritis" in her hips, i.e., phantom arthritis from an emotional scar caused by an unplanned scare. She told Jack he was a day late and a dime short because she already had developed arthritis in her hips. She hung up on him before he could get her number.

Kitty Klauson called next. She said her two boys, Rudy and Rebel, both had slivers, bruises, tetanus shots, stomachaches and you name it from the Scrap Lumber pile at school. She wanted to know if there was a chance there would be a quick settlement, and if so, would it be enough to buy her boyfriend a new fishing boat before Opener in May. This time it was Jack Shyster who hung up. It was a first for him.

Sven Nordquist called next and gave Jack a piece of his mind along with his philosophy about life. Jack Shyster patiently listened to Sven bang his cane against the phone. Sven was trying to yell above the shrill noise coming from his hearing aid. Jack Shyster thanked him, and told him if he ever needed his services for anything, just call. Sven hung up, dropped the phone, or dropped dead. Jack couldn't tell. He was glad to be off the phone with him.

The next week's edition of the local newspaper was boring (there wasn't even a domestic in the local police report), except for a new ad that appeared from the You Too Can Sleep Well at Night Insurance Company. It read: *Your friendly hometown insurance company can help you with all your needs. Whether you need Home, Auto, Health, Life, Hail, Wind, Flood or Scrap Lumber insurance, we'll take care of you.'* Of course, this ad was guaranteed to generate calls to the You Too Can Sleep Well at Night Insurance Company, and it sure did.

This time Sven Nordquist was the first to call. "That's it," he yelled over the loud, shrill sound his hearing aid was emitting. "I hope you're planning to give me a Senior Citizen discount if I have to insure my Scrap Lumber pile. Pretty soon I'm going to have no choice but to move back to Sweden." Sven hung up, dropped the phone, or dropped dead before Linda, the secretary, at the You Too Can Sleep Well at Night Insurance Company could respond.

Several others called too, mostly the oldtimers and the cognizant residents from the Rest O' Nod Nursing Home who called mid-morning when there was a lull in the day, after The Price is Right was over and before noon dinner was served. They wanted to know if Scrap Lumber insurance would affect their Medicare supplemental premiums. Linda, the head secretary at the You Too Can Sleep Well At Night Insurance Company, couldn't take it anymore. She gave her two-week notice and quit.

The month went by quickly and everyone was anxiously awaiting the City Council Meeting except Mayor Magnuson, the City Councilmen and Sheriff Art Schmidt. Mayor Magnuson was thankful that the weather had been so nice. He was hoping the locals would be so tired from raking and cleaning their yards that they'd just stay home. But, no such luck. Everyone who had been there the month before turned up again, except for Ben Bauer whom Mayor Magnuson assumed was too busy in the fields with the nice weather and all.

A new face showed up at City Hall, Jack Shyster from the 1-800-Gotchya Law Firm. Wearing a dark blue suit, white shirt, small print tie, polished wing tips, and carrying a black leather brief case under his arm, he looked as out of place at the City Council Meeting as Esther Larson would have looked if she had been sipping a Slow Gin Fizz and playing Canasta at the local VFW Lounge while wearing white go-go boots and three satin-bound, netted cancans under an above-the-knee red and white checkered square-dancing skirt that was paired with a white cotton blouse that had a draw-string neck and short elasticized sleeves.

Mayor Magnuson called the meeting to order and informed everyone in attendance that they were not at a Town Hall Meeting, but at a City Council Meeting and the Council would be voting on whether or not people had to get rid of their Scrap Lumber piles, not discussing it. "Now," he firmly said, "Is this clear to everyone?" Gracia Green and her people stood up. Penelope and her PETA people followed. In single file fashion they marched in front of the Mayor and the City Council Members with their protest signs and then left. Bud, the Bearded Local, who looked and smelled like he hadn't bathed or changed clothes since last month's meeting, yelled, "Good riddance to bad rubbish." Mayor Magnuson pounded his gavel, looked at Bud and said," I'm warning you. No outbursts."

Mayor Magnuson introduced Jack Shyster. He asked him to explain the laws on the books con-cerning Scrap Lumber piles, and any legal ramifi-cations that would result from either approving or denying Scrap Lumber piles. Jack walked to the front of the room, opened his brief case and said, "Good evening. I won't take long."

Sven Nordquist, whose hearing aid rang louder than the noon whistle, yelled, "Speak up, Sonny. I can't hear." Bud, the Bearded Local, chimed in, "And speak English while you're at it." Mayor Magnuson glared at Bud and said, "I've warned you once tonight. Now get out." Bud, the Bearded Local, got up, pointed to Jack Shyster, turned to the locals and said, "Watch him. I ain't never trusted anyone who wore a monkey suit, and you shouldn't either."

Bud left, but he wasn't finished. The windows were open and everyone heard a dog yipping and Penelope, the PETA leader, screaming. Sheriff Schmidt left the room for a few minutes. Then all was quiet and Sheriff Schmidt came back in.

Harley Davidson stood up, cleared his throat, rattled his thick silver chain and walked out. He reved his motorcycle for such a long time that the Sheriff went outside again. Harley drove away, Sheriff Schmidt came back in, and peace was restored — but not for long.

Mayor Magnuson apologized to Jack Shyster, and told him to continue. Serina Severson stood up and said, "You better not be one of those abortion lawyers, and if you are. . .". Mayor Magnuson nodded at Sheriff Schmidt who then got up, took Serina by the arm, and escorted her out. She was yelling as she was leaving but no one got upset because everyone had just assumed that Serina would be hauled out, too.

Mayor Magnuson took a drink of water and again apologized to Jack Shyster. Jack presented the legal issues and there were no further outbursts. Sven Nordquist had fallen asleep and was snoring so loudly that Sheriff Schmidt went and tapped him on the shoulder. Finally the vote was taken. The decision by the Mayor and the Council was that people could keep their Scrap Lumber piles as long as they kept them in their garages or outbuildings where no one could see them. The meeting was adjourned, but the Scrap Lumber issue wasn't over. It was just on hold.

That summer all was pretty quiet on the homefront because everyone was fishing and farming, but the dam broke open in September. The School Board was notified right before school opened in September that a class action suit was being filed by the 1-800-Gotchya Law firm against the local school district, the superintendent, the principals, the teachers, teacher aides, cooks, janitors, coaches, bus drivers, School Board Members, and the citizens who lived directly across from the school. The letter was signed by Jack Shyster.

The same letter was sent to the local lumber yard notifying them that the lumber yard, its owner, and the workers of the local lumber yard and their friends were also being sued in the class action suit.

The School District's Superintendent called their insurance representative at the You Too Can Sleep Well At Night Insurance Company to find out if they were protected. All they got was a busy signal and an operator saying, "Please hang up and try your call again."

The owner of the local lumber yard didn't have any better luck reaching the "You Too Can Sleep Well At Night Insurance Company. He personally drove down to their office but the doors were locked and a note on the door said, "Closed until further notice."

The local Walmart store was also being sued in the same lawsuit. Jack Shyster's law firm was well aware that Walmart had good insurance and deep pockets because they had successfully managed to get most of the local money away from the other businesses in town. Shyster realized that he was going out on a limb and on shaky grounds by going after Walmart for no good reason but he liked the thrill of gambling and put money on the idea that Walmart usually just paid up to save face and look good, so he took his chances.

Pretty soon everyone got involved. The two locals who were running against each other for the State House Representative seat each decided to make the Scrap Lumber issue their top political, hot potato issue. They even got on the local cable television show to debate the issue. Pretty soon, busybodies, law firms, insurance companies and politicians from the surrounding area got into the issue of Scrap Lumber, and it soon became the number one priority for everyone at the state level, even ahead of abortion, welfare reform, teachers' salaries, soaring medical costs, light rail transit, Jesse Ventura's playboy interview, and the height of deer stands up North.

The story got better. ABC, NBC and CBS got involved. To begin with it was only on the local nightly news, but soon the big three — Dan Rather, Peter Jennings, and Tom Brokaw – jumped in with both feet and opened their nightly newscasts with horror tales about Scrap Lumber. Ted Koppel on Nightline upended the big three and produced an hour-long Scrap Lumber documentary. Not to be outdone Barbara Walters of 60 Minutes interviewed Betty Busybody who had started the whole thing. Rush Limbaugh was calling it a leftist Communist pinko plot and his devoted listeners took him at his word. The candidate for the President of the United States who knew the most about Scrap Lumber won the election.

The President of the United States was pressured into dissolving the Department of Education and took the funds from education to create the

Department of Scrap Lumber. The Secretary of the Department of Scrap Lumber, Dresser Drawer (who everyone called Scrappy for short) was given a cabinet position and new office with cabinets made from mahogany Scrap Lumber. In no time at all, Scrap Lumber issues forced the unions to get involved. The AFL-CIO, became the AFL-CIO-SCRAP LUMBER. NAFTA rules and the issue of illegal dumping of Scrap Lumber got the mob involved. In no time at all Scrap Lumber became a black market commodity and the FBI got some more work.

The BBC picked the story up, and the issue of Scrap Lumber quickly became a global trade issue. The President of the United States called all the world leaders to a Global Summit Meeting in Yellowstone National Park. The CIA were invited came just in case. The leaders of the nations didn't get much accomplished but their wives, families and aides got a free trip out of the deal and had a chance to see Old Faithful erupt. The eruption reminded the Norwegian and Japanese Delegations of whales spouting off their coastlines, and the matter of whale-hunting became a side issue of the Summit. All of the delegates and leaders from the many nations went home rested, tanned, and with a personalized keychain carved from expensive teak Scrap Lumber as a souvenir token from this first Annual Worldwide Summit Meeting on Scrap Lumber.

Things kept spinning out of control. Regis Philbin started a new television show called, "Earn A Million Bucks By Being the Fastest Scrap Lumber Stacker." It was the top-watched show, even eclipsing the soaps and the President's State of the Union message to the nation. Time magazine wrote an article for the liberals about Scrap Lumber called, "Why Johnny Can't Read." CNN and FOX networks got their so-called experts to come on their news shows to debate the issue 24 hours day preempting Nash Bridges reruns. The producer of the Politically Incorrect show called in Hollywood stars so they could share their feelings, hairdos, and cleavage on such a hot topic, even though they really didn't care or know a thing about it. Jerry Springer jumped in with both feet and staged Scrap Lumber fights on his show, complete with flying chairs, blood, DNA tests, and infidelities. Sally Jesse Raphael got high ratings for her show entitled, "My Husband's About to Find Out that I'm Leaving Him for a Rugged Man who Saves Scrap Lumber and Wears Old Spice."

Stephen King wrote a horror story about a man who killed his wife and put her in a hollowed out tree in his front yard. Petrified as she had been, she soon petrified completely along with the tree. The killer sold the tree on e-Bay and made a fortune. So did Stephen King. Oprah nominated the book for her "You Got to Read This, It Speaks to Me Book Club" and it became a bestseller. The Coen brothers got into the action and produced a movie about it and the movie won Best Picture at the Academy Awards. Both a country western and a rap song were written about Scrap Lumber. They both soared to the top of the charts.

Scrap Lumber had hit the big time and became more and more commercial. The Mall of America had a store that only sold Scrap Lumber and Scrap Lumber paraphernalia.

Ralph Lauren and his Polo Club came out with a new line of Scrap Lumber sheets, towels and other linens. They were overpriced, but they were snapped up anyway by people who wanted the latest look. Target and Pier 1 came out with a line of college dorm furniture made of Scrap Lumber that not only looked good but was supposed to last for years, at least as many years (six to nine) as it would take to get a four-year degree. These companies knew they were safe in making the claim because kids don't hang onto anything that is over a year old.

Levi Strauss came out with a new line of jeans in Scrap Lumber Brown. They sold for $85.00 a pair and became so popular the company even made them in sizes big enough to fit the man who needed a little bit more room around the belly. They made them in Plus sizes for women who wanted to pretend they looked good in Levis.

McDonald's came out with a new Scrap Lumber burger for the man who wanted "to put some teeth in his meat." Coca-Cola put their coke in cans painted to look like Scrap Lumber and it became their top selling drink.

Calvin Klein had a new Scrap Lumber scent created called Scrap Lumber Spice. It was for the man who knows what a real smell was all about and it came out just in time for Father's Day. Packaged in Scrap Lumber boxes and tied with twine, it sold out in a few hours.

QVC made a mint selling Scrap Lumber jewelry, figurines and dolls by preying on hotflashing women who were up all night and had nothing better to do but sit and buy junk.

Martha Stewart developed a new paint color called Scrap Lumber Suede. It was kind of a muddy, gold-brown, baby poop shade that any thinking person wouldn't even bother to paint on the inside of a barn wall, but she was good at convincing the masses that it would turn their family rooms into showcases. She also created and sold a Scrap Lumber portable pickle dish to be used for picnics. Stay tuned; she'll think up more fluff.

People began to think, "What the heck. My pile might be worth something," so everyone started to hoard their Scrap Lumber piles. People were trading used boards through magazines and on e-Bay like they were baseball cards or Cabbage Patch Dolls. Rare and unusual Scrap Lumber pieces that commanded hundreds of thousands of dollars at Sotheby's Auction House got everyone frantically searching and sorting through their personal Scrap Lumber. Soon the New York Stock Exchange had a Scrap Lumber listing and everyone sold their tech stocks and bought Scrap Lumber Stocks so they could get rich fast and not have to wait for their money to grow on trees.

Pretty soon academia felt left out, but not for long. Classes on "The Sociological Development of Scrap Lumber from 1640-2000 and Its Impact on the Agricultural Society in the Northwest" were offered. These classes filled up fast, especially with athletes on full scholarships. More sections had to be added.

Almost every city began offering Community Education classes on "How to Sort and Maintain a Scrap Lumber Pile" for the men, and "Wooden Crafts To Delight" for the Mrs. to enroll in. These classes were offered at the same time on the same night so married couples could spend some quality time together, but when the adult students got home from class, they began fighting with their spouses over the best pieces of Scrap Lumber causing an outbreak of domestic violence. Boards of all sizes became weapons of destruction.

Psychiatrists made money counseling these married couples, and other people who felt left out of the Scrap Lumber loop. Doctors came up with a suspicious blood disease that was found only in Scrap Lumber collectors. Even though the Center for Disease and Control in Atlanta said it wasn't serious, the medical community made money off the tests, and drug companies made money off a new drug they developed that would cure it. People got tested for it even though they weren't quite sure what it was and they took the new drug as a preventative measure and because Medicare paid for it.

We could go on and on but the moral of the story is simple: *Anytime, anyone, anyplace makes a mountain out of a molehill, anyone and everyone can get a piece of the pile. It's the American Way.*

This is most certainly true.

CHAPTER FIFTEEN

CROSSWOOD PUZZLE: USES FOR SCRAP LUMBER

The Crosswood puzzle will be much
easier to figure out than this mess.

CrossWood Puzzle

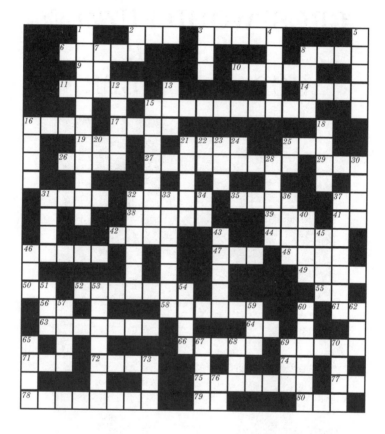

This "CrossWood" Puzzle is for the Retired Men who have their Scrap Lumber all in Order and are just waiting around to see the Great Scrap Lumber Pile in the Sky.

USES FOR SCRAP LUMBER

ACROSS

2. Scrap Lumber can be used by boys and frugal men to make floating fishing ____bers.

3. Scrap Lumber can be used to board up these parts of barn windows that have been broken by visually-challenged pigeons.

6. A race for young boys who have a penchant for pine.

8. Scrap Lumber can be used to patch one of these to keep rats out of the granary.

9. The patriarch who imparted the value of Scrap Lumber to his sons.

10. Scrap Lumber can be used to make a frame for this kind of garden crow.

11. A hunk of Scrap Lumber pounded over a mouse hole.

14. What Scrap Lumber frames in 8 Down.

15. Popular 4-H projects.

16. The county-wide event where 14 Across gets ribbons.

17. Marine batteries can rest ____ Scrap Lumber chunks during the winter months.

19. Saving Scrap Lumber is this kind of habit.

21. Skinny pieces of Scrap Lumber can be used to do this to a drum.

25. Scrap Lumber planks can be stacked to dry this crop.

26. Men sit outside and whittle Scrap Lumber while the Mrs. is getting her hair ____.

27. A nice Grandpa will make this out of Scrap Lumber for Sophia's playhouse.

29. If Mr.. Knutsvig's Scrap Lumber tips over, he might be in this kind of a wooden house.

31. Balsa Scrap Lumber can be used to make a frame for flying this.

32. Many long boards can be used to do this to keep a barn wall up.

35. A small piece of Scrap Lumber used to straighten things out or raise things up a little.

37. The person who has to look at and dust the Scrap Lumber that has been saved by 9 Across.

38. Scrap Lumber can be used to do this to a washing machine.

39. What Dick and Jane did on a seesaw made of long, sliver-free planks.

41. His wife told the neighbor, "Go find him. He's down ____ his precious Scrap Lumber pile."

42. A kind of bush held up by thin pieces of Scrap Lumber.

44. What men do to "No Hunting - No Trespassing" signs.

46. A cousin to a trunk-chewing rodent.

47. What the cattle did by the manger made from Scrap Lumber at the Sunday School Christmas program.

48. A "negative" part in some pine boards.

49. Leftover Scrap Lumber that came from around windows.

50. Scrap Lumber boards were used for making goal posts when this famous football player was young.

52. These mark pets' graves.

55. Crossword abbreviation for Down.

56. "____ least you could put a privacy fence around that pile of Scrap Lumber."

58. Foot-long pieces of old wood used as garden row markers.

61. She gave her man an ultimatum: "There's not room for both the Scrap Lumber pile and me. The pile will have to ____ or I will!"

63. There wouldn't be so much Scrap Lumber in the world if men had done this before they cut it.

64. He's got almost every kind of Scrap Lumber ____ that pile.

66. Chickens do this on horizontal pieces of Scrap Lumber.

69. Wooden ramps are made by boys so they can have these for their bikes.

71. Pine _____ oak are the most common kinds of Scrap Lumber.

72. A kind of box held up on a scrap post at the end of the driveway.

74. With the kids raised and gone, its just the Scrap Lumber pile and ___.

75. What a block of Scrap Lumber does to furniture when the basement starts to flood.

77. A curved piece of Scrap Lumber can be used as a yoke for this animal.

78. What Grandma used Scrap Lumber for in the cookstove.

79. The motto of most women is: _____ More Scrap Lumber!

80. Sticky stuff that might still be on a piece of maple Scrap Lumber.

DOWN

1. Scrap Lumber can be used to do this in an emergency to get from an island to the dock on the mainland in leaky vessels.

2. The most common board size is a 2 ____ 4.

3. Scrap Lumber can be used to make one of these for pigs.

4. The wooden part of swings.

5. George Washington had wooden ones.

7. The "finky" rodent involved in 8 Across.

8. The gender of poultry that has nests boxed in with Scrap Lumber.

12. An adjective describing homemade wooden decoy heads.

13. Men think that wasting Scrap Lumber would be a ___.

15. Burning piles of Scrap Lumber that are lit just before the Snake Dance at Homecoming.

16. Scrap Lumber used as sideboards for pouring cement.

18. What Mrs. Knutsvig yelled when she saw a pile of crooked Scrap Lumber, "Ny ____!"

20. ____ oak tree is too lovely to make Scrap Lumber from.

21. Another name for a 2 x 4 leaning against a gate.

22. How to say "One" in Norwegian, and it's not "*ett.*"

23. What you do with a bow and arrow before you shoot it at a birds-eye painted on a hunk of Scrap Lumber.

24. Abbreviation for "Tiny Toys" made with Scrap Lumber.

25. Pronoun for a typical Scrap Lumber stacker.

28. An upright plank of Scrap Lumber will do this to the clothesline so the Mrs. can hang out "overalls" and blankets.

30. An annoying insect that bothers you when you are cutting up Scrap Lumber outside.

31. Lars and _____ were good lumberjacks.

32. Chunks of Scrap Lumber placed under jacks to get the proper height.

33. Where skateboarders put Scrap Lumber ramps if they aren't placed in streets.

34. The phonetic abbreviation for Scrap Lumber would be "es" "__".

36. Scrap shingles can be used to do this to the traps at gopher holes.

37. What is placed under the glass, but over the picture edges, in a wooden picture frame.

40. Scrap Lumber stakes can be used to hang a blanket over the clothesline to make this.

43. A long piece of Scrap Lumber put over an old oil barrel used by Dick and Jane for a seesaw.

45. A measurement for firewood.

46. She put an ad in the paper and said "Huge Scrap Lumber Pile For Sale. $25.00 _____."

51. Coordinated, clever men can make shelves from Scrap Lumber to hold the Mrs.'s jars of this.

53. A clever Norwegian-Lutheran woman will do this to wooden signs marking the outhouses behind

the church.

54. A thin piece of Scrap Lumber can be used to do this to paint.

57. If a shepherd doesn't have a proper crook, he can use a Scrap Lumber pole to _____ his sheep.

59. What men do in their deer stands made out of Scrap Lumber.

60. Boys build these in trees out of Scrap Lumber.

62. When men see a really nice pile of Scrap Lumber they let out a bunch of _____ and Ahs.

65. Flat pieces of Scrap Lumber are used to _____ where the kitten ball bases are.

67. Short pieces of wood can prop old windows so they stay _____.

68. Mabel told her neighbor lady, "I can't even _____ the shed because of that dreadful Scrap Lumber pile."

69. A long board that sticks out of a nicely stacked Scrap Lumber pile can be said to do this.

70. What you can do with a plank to keep the Old Man upright.

73. What pirates used a hunk of Scrap Lumber for.

76. " _____ and behold, he's got more Scrap Lumber!"

CrossWood Puzzle
Answers

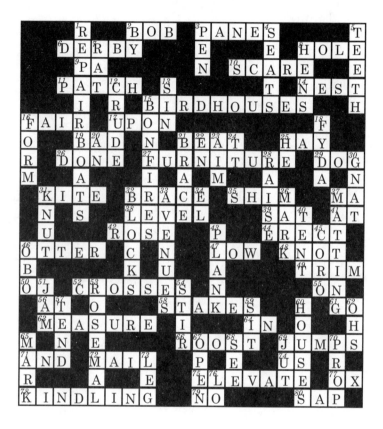

CHAPTER SIXTEEN

SCRAP LUMBER PHOTO OP

A picture is worth a thousand words!

She says:

"It's either me or this crap!"
"No, there's no place in the Bible that talks
    about something like this."
"I'm going inside to pray for a lightning bolt."
"What's Rapture to you, is Armageddon to me."

She says:

"No, it's not the same as saving scraps of fabric.
      Skunks don't burrow under fabric."
"What do you mean you're going to Home Depot?"
"Ever heard of the Untouchables?"
"I don't care what your mom put up with! I'm me,
      got it?"

She says:

"Take a garbage pail full of Scrap Lumber to the dump every week. He'll never notice. Trust me!"

She says:

"I wish he would wrap my Christmas gift as nice as he does his Scrap Lumber heap."

He says:

"It makes perfect sense!"
"Of course, it's logical!"
"Think of the wooden nickels I could make!"
"Well, Bob Vila has more spare time."
"Burn it? There's lots of good oak in the pile."
"When I retire..."

Hiding places for Scrap Lumber

The back of the garage.

The side of the garage.

Emergency pile of Scrap Lumber

Hunks of Scrap Lumber from the emergency pile put to good use.

Just look what the Mr. can
make with Fudgesickle sticks
when he retires.

ABOUT THE AUTHORS

Janet Letnes Martin - native of Hillsboro, ND and now a resident of Hastings, MN - and Suzann (Johnson) Nelson - who grew up near Evansville, MN and now lives in Grand Rapids, MN - met at Augsburg College in Minneapolis. They have both been married for years to Scandinavian rural men who save Scrap Lumber; Janet to Neil, and Suzann to Ron. They are both mothers and mothers-in-law. Janet's children are Jennifer (who is married to Steve Green), Sarah and Katrina. Suzann's children are Senja (who is married to Chris Morgue) and Siri. Janet is also delighted to be a grandmother to Sophia Linnea and is waiting for hundreds of more grandchildren.

Martin has co-authored several bestselling humor books with Allen Todnem: Cream and Bread, Second Helpings of Cream and Bread, and Lutheran Church Basement Women. In 1996 she compiled a heritage cookbook with her sister, Ilene Lorenz, called Our Beloved Sweden: Food, Faith, Flowers and Festivals. Martin has written Shirley Holmquist and Aunt Wilma; Who Dunit?, and Helga Hanson's Hotflash Handbook. She has also designed several humorous products: *Helga Hanson's Hotflash Hanky*, *Red Jell-O Queens' Dishtowels*, *Egg Coffee Mugs*, *Lutheran Hotdish Trivets*, and *Lutheran Jell-O Power Aprons*.

Nelson officially teamed up with Martin in 1994. Since then they have written Cream Peas on Toast: Comfort Food for Norwegian-Lutheran Farm Kids and Others; a Catholic- Lutheran Lexicon called They Glorified Mary, We Glorified Rice; and a Farm kids-Town kids Lexicon entitled They Had Stores, We had Chores. In 1996 Martin and Nelson wrote and published Uffda, But Those Clip-ons Hurt, Then! and a compendium of rural Midwestern farm phrases entitled, Is It Too Windy Back There, Then?

Next they wrote their award winning book Growing Up Lutheran: What Does This Mean?, a winner of the Minnesota Book Award for Humor. The book is also available as a book-on-tape. In 1998 they began performing stand-up comedy with their first major booking at the Medora Musical. An audio cassette entitled, *Those Lutheran Ladies*, recorded live, followed. In 1999 they wrote Luther's Small Dictionary: From AAL to Zululand, an extension of their book, Growing Up Lutheran.

In this new century, Martin and Nelson have written this hilarious book and developed a teeshirt and cap to go with it.

Martin, her son-in-law and daughter, Steve and Jennifer Green, run a mail-order catalog and have a Scandinavian retail store, **Scandinavian Marketplace**. It is located at 218 East 2nd St. Hastings, MN, 55033. They can be reached by calling 1-800-797-4319, or on by e-mail at steve@scandinavianmarket.com. Their website is located at: www.scandinavianmarketplace.com.

Nelson has edited many books, including Our Beloved Sweden. She is the sole distributor of Erling Rolsrud's prairie books. She also has a mail-order book catalog called Rural Route Bookstore. It is available through **Noteworthy Press** at 910

NW 9th St., Grand Rapids, MN, 55744. She can be reached at 1-800-494-9124.

Martin and Nelson, individually or together, are very much in demand as speakers. Their humorous presentations are centered around their experiences growing up in rural Norwegian-American Lutheran communities. To book either or both of the authors for speaking engagements, contact Jennifer Green at 651-437-5268 or at: lutheranladies@aol.com.

ORDER BLANK

Name _____

Address_____

City_____State_____Zip_____

Telephone #_____-_____-_____

_____ Scrap Lumber **book**: @ $9.95   Subtotal $_____

#_____ Scrap Lumber **hat**: @ $16   Subtotal $_____

Scrap Lumber **teeshirts**:
Size M____   L ____or   XL____ @ $16   Subtotal $_____
Size XXL ____   XXXL___ @ $17   Subtotal $_____

Plus shipping and handling:
      Up to $10.00 = $3.95
      Up to $20.00 = $4.95
      Up to $30.00 = $5.95
      Up to $40.00 = $6.95
      Up to $50.00 = $7.95
      Up to $60.00 = $8.95
      Above $60.00 = $9.95   S&H $_____

MN residents add 6.5%
(Sales tax on book only, not clothes)   Sales Tax $_____

                                        Total $_____

Send check, money order, Visa or Mastercard # to:

CARAGANA PRESS
PO BOX 396,
HASTINGS, MN 55033

Visa or Mastercard #_____ Exp._____

TO ORDER BY PHONE OR INTERNET:
CALL (800) 797-4319 or www.scandinavianmarketplace.com for
these products, other books and products, and for Janet's catalog.

CALL (800) 494-9124 or e-mail: snelson.uslink.net to order these
products, other books and products and for Suzann's catalog.

(Note: Our catalogs are different and both are worth the call.)

ORDER BLANK

Name _____

Address_____

City_____State_____Zip_____

Telephone #_____-_____-_____

_____ Scrap Lumber **book**: @ $9.95   Subtotal $_____

#_____ Scrap Lumber **hat**: @ $16   Subtotal $_____

Scrap Lumber **teeshirts**:
Size M____   L ___or   XL___ @ $16   Subtotal $_____
Size XXL ____   XXXL___ @ $17   Subtotal $_____

Plus shipping and handling:
      Up to $10.00 = $3.95
      Up to $20.00 = $4.95
      Up to $30.00 = $5.95
      Up to $40.00 = $6.95
      Up to $50.00 = $7.95
      Up to $60.00 = $8.95
      Above $60.00 = $9.95   S&H $_____

MN residents add 6.5%
(Sales tax on book only, not clothes)   Sales Tax $_____

                           Total $_____

Send check, money order, Visa or Mastercard # to:

CARAGANA PRESS
PO BOX 396,
HASTINGS, MN 55033

Visa or Mastercard #_____ Exp._____

TO ORDER BY PHONE OR INTERNET:
CALL (800) 797-4319 or www.scandinavianmarketplace.com for
these products, other books and products, and for Janet's catalog.

CALL (800) 494-9124 or e-mail: snelson.uslink.net to order these
products, other books and products and for Suzann's catalog.

(Note: Our catalogs are different and both are worth the call.)